How to Lose Your Ass and Regain Your Life

Reluctant Confessions of a Big-Butted Star

Kirstie Alley

Notice

Mention of specific companies, organizations, or authorities in this book does not imply endorsement by the publisher, nor does mention of specific companies, organizations, or authorities imply that they endorse this book.

Internet addresses and telephone numbers given in this book were accurate at the time it went to press.

Printed in the United States of America
Rodale Inc. makes every effort to use acid-free ♾, recycled paper ♻.

Book design by Joanna Williams

Library of Congress Cataloging-in-Publication Data on file with publisher

Distributed to the book trade by Holtzbrinck Publishers

2 4 6 8 10 9 7 5 3 1 hardcover

RODALE
LIVE YOUR WHOLE LIFE™

We inspire and enable people to improve their lives and the world around them

For more of our products visit **rodalestore.com** or call 800-848-4735

Lillie and True, this book is for you
For whenever you're cuckoo
Or just feeling blue
The errors of your mother
Need never infect you . . .
So just read ahead
And learn what not *to do.*

Love,
Mama

THANK YOU

Robert Alley, Lillian Maxine Heaton, Collette, Craig, all my cousins, aunts, uncles, and grandparents. All pets, past and present, ex-husbands, ex-boyfriends, good friends, old and new and, of course, Mr. L. Ron Hubbard, who turned out to be the most helpful friend I've ever had.

A special shout-out to Peggy Crawford. Your nimble typing fingers, bountiful patience, and astute attention were vital. Thank you for taking months of your valuable time to assist me by calming the waters and steadying the course so that I could write this book.

And last, but certainly not least, to all you big-bottomed girls out there who are not always treated like queens.

THANK YOU for making the boat I'm in a little less lonely, and THANK YOU for inspiring me to hopefully inspire all of us. Hail, hail the Queens of Posterior, the big-bottomed girls who have then, now, and always RULED!

Thank you.

Contents

My journey was never intended to end like this.

Little did I know when I plotted to become a modern-day "Donna Reed," that I was in fact plotting the prelude to my own physical demise. A simple decision, really—a choice to create a more beautiful life for my children—somehow took a sharp left turn, ending up in the twilight zone of lard.

It all sounded so swell. A stay-at-home mother. Heartfelt vows made to cook more fancy meals, to rustle up more pretty cupcakes, to attend more kid parties, movies, ice cream stores, and grade school functions.

It did sound swell. It did. It was such a perfectly laid, then executed scheme. Very "correct." Very "1947." Very "we'll all go to heaven."

The ironic part of it is, I did achieve my goal. I did become the most effective, life-loving, children-pleasing, hands-on mother that I could possibly become. I could never and would never regret that.

It was just the ass thing—the ass thing is what threw me for a loop.

My ass became an independent entity. As my love and hands-on-ness grew, so grew IT. So grew my alternate personality'd ample rump.

It's sort of like the reverse vector of an unsuccessful liposuction surgery—all that nasty yellow fat sucked away from the trusting patient's fluffy body. But—oops—the patient is dead. Indeed, I flowed all my love and attention to my luscious, beloved children. But—oops—my ass had engulfed my body, overwhelming it to such a degree that it seemed no one could see ME anymore.

Will the real slim Kirstie please stand up? Please stand up?

I needed to call OnStar to re-route my journey. I needed a spiritual and physical overhaul. A reckoning, so to speak—with my ever-expanding, unidentifiable flying object of a bottom.

An on-course, new journey that would once and for all answer the universal female question:

"Is it possible to live a beautiful life and also maintain a decent-sized *ASS?*"

This is OUR question . . .

This is OUR journey . . .

Kirstie Louise Alley

1

Little Suede Pants

December 31st, 2003

New Year's Eve in Wichita, Kansas. Ass size of neighboring state, Oklahoma. Children flown to Los Angeles to have New Year's with their father. Ate massive quantities of Santa-head frosted sugar cookies, cheese fondue, steak tartare, Key lime pie, homemade chicken and noodles, with Cinnabon chaser, and 50 or 60 other mystery foods. Then went to dinner.

Went to Vietnamese restaurant, "Ah-So." Watched old movies on Turner Classic Network, reflected on how body got whalelike. How men were not falling over me in last year.

Wondered if new family had clandestinely moved into ass over holidays.

Big New Year's resolution—to find new way to reduce ass and to recreate once-beautiful life. Also, to look for prospect to have sex with in future.

Oh, and also, to close piehole long enough to at least identify food particles passing into it.

Seven hundred and fifty dollars was the price tag of the little suede pants that were tugging at my heartstrings. They were fawn-colored, slightly rough suede, with long fringe all the way from waist to ankle on the outside seams. Low-cut, lined with buckskin-colored silk, size two.

I had gotten my first movie and was paid a little money, so although $750 was still outside my price range, I knew I would not go without food, as I'd done in the past when something had stricken my fancy.

I had an enormous crush on an actor from the movie *Animal House*. We'll just call him Tim Matheson . . . because that is his name.

Tim and I had had several odd dates. When I look back on it, I believe I was the "don't-really-have-another-date-so-call-her" girl.

At times it seemed we were quite smitten with each other, but he was never as smitten with me as I was with him. I don't usually name names when I recall stories from my past, but after what Tim did, I consider him fair game.

Tim had asked me out for New Year's Eve. Now, this was a huge step in our weird relationship; New Year's Eve is a coveted date slot, and we girls are no dummies—we know the significance of a New Year's Eve date.

My hair was very long, to the middle of my back. I weighed 114 pounds. I'd been working out regularly. All 5 feet 8 inches of me was fine.

Tim called—Did I want to go out the night before New Year's Eve also? It was his birthday, the eve before New Year's Eve. Okay, now I was not the gangster of love, I was not the expert of trysts, but wow, the night before New Year's Eve, his birthday, then New Year's Eve? And he had said, yeah, then let's go somewhere New Year's Day.

It seemed that old Timmy boy had fallen as hard as I had. It seemed inevitable that it was only a matter of time before I became Mrs. Animal House, Mrs. Tim.

Tim and I actually looked like brother and sister. Both of us had dark hair and light eyes and black lashes and brows. Both tall, good teeth, nice smiles. Our Animal House children would, without a doubt, look like clones of us, as we looked like clones of each other.

I went back to the little suede pant shop and re-splurged on a sweater to accompany the little suede pants. It was a sort of raspberry-colored mohair with raspberry-colored fox fur inset into the shoulders of the sweater—remember this was the 80s; shoulder pads ruled. But these raspberry, fox-adorned shoulders didn't need pads. They were so fluffy on their own that they achieved double shoulder pad status. My flat, hard, tan stomach peeked out from the 2-inch gap between raspberry sweater and little suede pants.

Raspberry fox sweater? $545.

Then there were those boots I'd seen at Fred Segal's. Raspberry kid-leather 4-inch heels, inside zipper from ankle to knees. Raspberry boots—$375.

Underwear—raspberry lace bra and bikini pants, add an additional 200 bucks. Perfume, the only kind I wore back then was Casaque—clean and yet hauntingly sexy.

Tim did not have to pick me up for his birthday date, pre–New Year's Eve date, as Tim lived next door to me. That's sort of how I met Tim, that's what we really had most in common—our addresses.

Chestnut, perfectly waved and ringletted hair down my back, raspberry fur sex sweater, little suede pants, raspberry killer boots with 4-inch heels, yummy lingerie, and sensual scented Casaque—that all topped off with tons of black, Bridget Bardot eyeliner and pale, very pale titty-pink lip gloss. No wonder Animal House was hot on my trail. Damn booty! I was one of Hollywood's finest up-and-coming ingénues, although I was 30 years old. I was definitely up and coming, and everyone thought I was 23 anyway.

I strolled next door to Tim's. We had champagne and laughed that giddy champagne laughter. He took me out to dinner and then, of course, we came back to his place. Tim and I were pretty excellent lovers really—no trouble getting on the same wavelength. Tim lit a fire in his bedroom. It was a funny house—his bedroom was upstairs, but the only thing upstairs *was* the bedroom, so if you went to the top of the staircase, it just opened into his bedroom. No halls, no guest rooms, just one big bedroom with a master bath attached. It was a tricked-out expensive house.

Tim had worked a lot and was not short on funds. It was unlike the small house that my two roommates and I rented next door. Tim's house was the pièce de résistance of the block, and it also had a lot of land, I'd say about 3 acres.

As I stood in front of his fireplace in his upstairs-only bedroom, I stealthily peeled off my raspberry fox sweater, then unzipped my little suede pants and pulled them over my kid-leather, raspberry 4-inch-heeled fuck me boots. There I stood, raspberry boots, bra, and bikini—raspberries took on a whole new meaning.

Tim and I made passionate love, then Tim served up a tray of fine pastries from Michele Richard. We decadently lay there dining on éclairs, napoleons, and petit fours. It was 30 minutes until midnight—30 minutes until Animal House became a year older.

Suddenly I got a weird feeling in my gut. Not like an "I've just been laid" feeling—no, something much different. A sort of nervousness, like when my mother had been killed in a car wreck. I excused myself to the restroom. I was pacing about for a while, trying to figure out why I was nervous, yet still noticing my fabulous, just laid, tossled hair trailing down almost to my waist. I thought, *Damn, I look good after sex, damn!*

I looked outside the window and noticed that I could see my roommate Callie talking on the phone in our house next door. It made me laugh—here I was naked and had just been banged, and there she was yapping away on the phone to God knows who, slurping down a diet Coke with lime. I tapped on Tim's window to try to get her attention, stupidly thinking she would hear me and look up. She didn't, and she didn't. I had calmed down a little bit, and didn't feel quite so anxious, so I went back into the bedroom to be with Animal House. Five minutes until showtime. Five minutes until Tim's birthday.

I sat on the edge of his bed naked, Barbarella hair'd and all. He lay on the bed naked with my hair cascading down his chest.

"Tim," I said. "I think I should go home, I feel a little weird."

"Oh, come on, Kirstie," he said. "It's almost midnight, it's almost my birthday. Stay all night with me, let's make love again as my birthday present."

One minute 'til midnight.

Oh Tim, oh Animal House, oh you black-haired, blue-eyed God of college girls everywhere—of course I'll stay and birthday fuck your brains out. I'm falling in love with you, Animal House, truly I am, and you've become awfully interested in me lately. Of course I'll stay; hell, I'll stay forever and ever. I can watch my ex-roommate Callie talking on the phone each night out our bathroom window in my old rented house next door!

We began to kiss a deep, hot, desperate kiss of young, deep, hot, desperate lovers. Bong, bong, bong . . . bong, bong, bong. . . . The clock downstairs in Tim's living room struck midnight. I came up for air.

"Happy birthday, baby—happy birthday."

Yes, Tim was riveted on me, mesmerized by my wonderfulness. I had him in my tight little grasp. He was quivering, smitten with my majestic beauty and expert lovemaking.

Just then I heard something way out of context. Knock, knock, knocking on heaven's door.

"Tim," this voice said.

"Dora," Tim nervously blurted out.

I sat up and turned my body to the left. There stood this beautiful red-haired girl.

"Tim" she said, more desperately.

"Dora!" he said more horrifyingly.

It was a very bad rendition of George and Marsha.

I decided, as I was between Dora (we'll call her Dora) and Animal House, to go invisible. So, I did. I just made myself invisible. I disappeared into another dimension.

God, Tim, say something besides "Dora" for Christ's sake. Say, hey, get outta here—say, who the hell are you? Or what are you doing in my house? Say something, say something, I can't stay invisible much longer.

Dora ran down the stairs in a burst of hysteria and screaming, "Oh, my God, oh my God, how could you do this?" Tim was up in a flash, putting his jeans on frantically.

He said, "Stay here, don't leave."

Hmm . . . Stay here, don't leave?

Remember, there was only one way to get downstairs. Was I going to leisurely saunter down the stairs to greet a hysterical

Dora who would possibly pull out a knife and murder me?

Yes, Timmy boy, I'll most certainly stay right here, but hey . . . who in the hell is Dora, anyway?

I put my raspberry lingerie on, my raspberry mohair fox-trimmed sweater, my soft kidskin raspberry 4-inch heeled boots, and finally my beloved little suede pants, with the delicate long strips of suede fringe dripping down from my thighs to my ankles.

I could make out some of what pretty Dora was saying, "engaged." Engaged was the word that specifically stuck in my mind. And "how the fuck could you cheat on me like this?" was another showstopper.

Tim screaming, "I'm sorry, I'm sorry, calm down, I'm sorry." Dora was screaming at the top of her beautiful strawberry lungs, then she ran outside and her wails trailed off.

A perfect time for my exit, I thought. I'll just run down the stairs, out of the house, and quickly fly inside my rented house. I began my descent, but whoa, Dora was back. The wailing was coming closer and closer.

Damn! They were back in the house. I hauled ass back up the stairs into Tim's little "infidelity" love nest.

This scenario occurred over and over—in and out, in and out of the house Dora went like some misguided cuckoo clock. I became desperate, choking for oxygen. It was surely only a matter of time before Dora went totally psychotic and decided to take her pain out on the bitch upstairs who was screwing her fiancé!

It turned out that beautiful Dora was actually engaged to Animal House and that she had traveled all the way from New York City to stand in her betrothed's front yard and wait until the clock struck midnight, then bound in and wish Tiny Tim a happy birthday! How the hell any chick could or would trust ole Timmy boy is beyond me, but apparently Mrs. Soon-to-Be Tim had, in fact, truly believed that he would just be waiting like a good little boy on a Saturday night, all snuggled in his footie jammies drinking hot chocolate and eating animal crackers.

And what about him? Did it not occur to him that his fiancée would at least be giving him a call on his birthday? And what the hell was he going to say he was doing the next night, New Year's Eve? Out with the boys? Home in bed again? What?

Oh God, I had to get out of there, and quick. I ran to the bathroom and looked out the window. Callie was still on the phone. A solution hit me like a ton of bricks. I'll have Callie bring a ladder over, and I'll go out the bathroom window while Dora is wailing in the living room. Yes, yes, good plan. Good plan, Kirstie, good thinking even under extreme duress.

854-3317—beep, beep, beep, beep. Damn, busy, of course busy, I can see her mouth moving for Christ's sake. Okay, emergency breakthrough, that's it.

"Hello, yes operator, I'd like to make an emergency interrupt to 854-3317. Yes, I'll hold. I'll hold."

The operator says, "I'm sorry, the party will not give up the line."

And why wouldn't the party? Callie, Terry, and I each made at least three emergency interrupts a day, trying to get the other of us to hang up the damn phone!

"Operator, please try again, please tell the party this is a *real* emergency—a *real* emergency and I must get through."

Operator: "I'm sorry, the party says they are in the middle of a conversation with a new hot guy and will not be able to give up the line at this time."

Fuck you, Callie, fuck you, fuck you, fuck you! Can't you see me in this window? Can't you tell a real emergency call from the countless fake emergency calls we make during the day? It's midnight, for fuck's sake. No one makes fake emergency calls at midnight, you fucking idiot!

How far down is it anyway? If I jumped, I mean. Would I break something or only sprain something? Let's see, Dora murdering me or a slightly sprained something—okay, I'll go with the sprain.

Open the window, shimmy out little suede pants, hang on tight, lower, lower, lower. Thud! Raspberry kid-leather boots 4-inch heels, sucked 4 inches into the sod below, cushioned the blow. But hard to pry those 4 inches out of the mud. Damn, one heel broken at the quick—shit! Raspberry mohair fox-shouldered sweater—snagged on a holly bush. Stretched way, way out. Look to the left, look to the right, no Dora, no Animal House, hobble for my life next door.

Hobble, hobble, hobble, door locked. Oh shit, door locked and purse is still in Tim's love den—shit!

Around the side of the house to Callie's window—bam, bam, bam, bam, Callie! Loud whisper-scream so Dora will not hear me and come over yonder and beat the shit out of me.

I hear Callie, "Oh God, I've gotta get off the phone and call the police—someone is outside." Still pounding on the glass, wondering if blondes do have lower IQs.

Around to the front door. Ding dong, ding dong, ding dong. As I peer into the entry hall door, I see Callie crouched on the floor calling the police. *Oh God, Callie, you can't be this stupid, you really can't.*

Around to the back of the house I ran. Maybe we'd left the back door unlocked as usual. As I ran to the back door, the inevitable occurred—not Dora as I'd expected, no, something more lethal to little suede pants.

The sprinklers went off.

The sprinklers sprinkled my little suede pants until they were drenched and cold and sagged around my oh-so-perfect, size-two booty—like poopy diapers on a toddler.

The back door was unlocked. The police were called off. Dora went back into Animal House's house and all was quiet this birthday eve. This eve of New Year's Eve.

Tim came over the next day and explained a few things, including that he didn't really think it "appropriate" to have our New Year's Eve date now with Dora and the engagement and all.

You think so, mother fucker? You really think it "inappropriate"?

Tim and Dora were soon unengaged, I heard, and I was soon in love with another actor, trading Animal House in for a Hardy Boy.

Cut to 17 years later.

I'm auditioning actors to play my husband on *Veronica's Closet*. I was the producer of *Veronica's Closet* and the star of *Veronica's Closet*, and stars of shows have the choice of all the other lead actors surrounding them.

"Next," the casting director announced.

"Next up is . . . Tim Matheson, send Tim in."

"Yes," I said with a maniacal "here's Johnny" smirk on my face.

"Yes, please . . . please do send Tim, Tim, Timmy Tim in, yes, pleeease do.

"Moo ha ha, moo ha ha!"

Lesson learned: Make sure dates are not married or engaged, carry an umbrella, and watch out for sprinklers!

2

Lillian's Diet

January 12th, 2004

My birthday. Got call from accountant. Between our combined errors . . . oops, owe IRS huge amount of extra taxes.

Noticed I was fat, ugly, and old. Now, fat, ugly, old, and poor. Ate nothing. Hid in bed under covers for next 5 days, lost 8 pounds. Birthday present to self.

January 17th, 2004

When head peeked out of covers, decided to confront IRS mess. Decided to go get Scientology session to keep self from imploding.

Biggest decision—decided to wash hair.

January 18th, 2004

Made decision in session to stop being victim. Came up with plan. Sell this, move that, collect on outstanding loans to friends, tap savings.

Good, IRS handled. Will not have to spend Easter in federal penitentiary.

Gained back 8 pounds lost during IRS depression, by celebrating IRS solutions with giant feast at Chi Dynasty and whole box of rice crackers smeared with globs of French butter. Pretended French butter was special 15-calorie V-8 spread. Realized have major situation with excess and life view of "more is better."

Need to get grip on next half of life. Need to have revelation on purpose of food.

I came from the "clean your plate" generation. Clean your plate was a hard-and-fast rule for everyone in my house, except my mother. My mother . . . skinny as a rail with the most beautiful legs I've ever seen. Like Betty Grable, only better.

Lillian Maxine Heaton was a tiny thing, about 5 foot 2, but perfectly proportioned. If you saw a picture of her, you wouldn't be able to tell if she was 5 foot 2 or 5 foot 8.

Now her diet was very interesting. A shining example for me if I ever desired to be svelte, perfectly proportioned with Betty Grable legs.

Coffee. Coffee beginning at 7:00 A.M., swigged down before, during, and after we were off to school and right up until we came home at noon.

My mother was basically the neighborhood "counselor." We left for school and one or more of her "patients" would drop by for life advice.

Around noon, she would exchange the coffee for Coca-Colas. In our house we were allowed one soft drink and one soft drink only—Coca-Cola. In fact, we had a "Coke man." He delivered cases and cases of Coke to the house weekly. If I asked for 7-Up or Orange Crush or, God forbid, Pepsi-cola, I would get the same choreographed mantra, "We drink Cokes—we do not drink 7-Up, Orange Crush, or Pepsi-cola. The people who drink Pepsi are the same people who drive Buicks. We don't drive Buicks and we don't drink Pepsi. We drink Coke and we drive Chryslers and DeSotos."

My mother spoke in a very assertive manner. As sure as President Eisenhower spoke of the Cold War, my mother spoke of Coca-Cola and models of cars.

My personal favorite drink was actually grape Kool-Aid. But my mother made it clear that Kool-Aid was a poor people's drink, and that we were middle class and thus we didn't have to drink Kool-Aid, we could afford Coca-Colas. Apparently my mother went to the Harvard School of, "I'm gonna make up any shit I want to and make you think I know what I'm talking about."

Nevertheless, my new mantra was, "When I grow up, I shall not be poor. I shall force myself to hate grape Kool-Aid, and I shall display my Coca-Colas like Emmys so that all will be aware that I am rich—or at least middle class."

While we ate Campbell's soup for lunch—my favorite was chicken with rice, and still is—Lillian Maxine, "Mickey," would eat half a peanut butter, banana, and sugar sandwich spread on, what else, white Wonder bread. This, of course, was washed down with a what? A Coca-Cola.

I don't remember having anything for lunch other than a variation of the Campbell's soup menu. I once commented to Lillian after dining at a friend's house for lunch that her mother had served us turkey sandwiches, homemade noodle soup, and garnishes of radish rosettes that she had hand-carved.

Lillian's response:

"I don't really give a rat's ass what Lynn's mother made. I don't have enough goddamn time to carve rosettes for you goddamn kids!" And rightly so. How could she possibly have accommodated her many morning "patients" if she was off gallivanting around the kitchen, brewing homemade soup and sculpting radishes?

If you were to open most drawers in our house, you would have come across my mother's mid-morning, mid-afternoon, and late night snacks. Hidden with the finesse of the Easter bunny were nests of peanut M&Ms, Milky Ways, and her most coveted Hershey bars. I figure that by 3:00 in the afternoon, my mother's daily consumption of sugar was equal to the 24-hour period following Halloween for most 10-year-old children.

I don't remember being offered snacks after school. I do remember making bread and butter and sugar sandwiches for myself. If I was really lucky, I'd fold in some marshmallow creme left over from my mother's batch of fudge.

It was usually my job to set the table for dinner. I didn't do well with doing dishes. My knees would buckle when my hands were in hot water too long. I would grow dizzy and nauseated and almost faint. So setting the table and cleaning all the bathrooms became my fate.

Several times while setting the table with Melmac plates and one tea towel in the middle for the entire family to use as a napkin, I would comment that I wished we could use the good china my mother had gotten for a wedding present.

I thought it was so beautiful. And I thought that if I set the table with those beautiful rose-covered plates and the hand-etched crystal beside it, we would all feel a little more special when we dined on pork chops that had been cooked for 2 hours (because "Jews know something we don't, and you have to cook pork chops until they bow up like taco shells or you will get Salmonella or trichinosis").

I thought Lillian would praise me for my ingenious idea to set a table that even Emily Post would marvel at. Instead, my mother's loving voice lilted across the kitchen:

"No! I don't want you to use the goddamn china. And who do you think you are anyway, the goddamn Queen of England? If the shit we use everyday isn't good enough for you, why don't you just move out of this goddamn house and go live in England?"

Never have I heard such profound advice.

How could I have been so stupid? Who *did* I think I was? The Queen?

As I ate my rubber pork chops and canned new potatoes that evening, I secretly thought to myself, *I would rather be a queen and eat off china plates than a lunatic who ate off Melmac.*

After the dishes were done, we had a family ritual. My father made popcorn drenched in beautiful yellow golden butter. My Mom got out the Snickers and M&Ms, and we kids brought down the Coca-Colas.

We all munched away on our sugar and butter and swigged down our middle-classed Coca-Colas, while Mom and Dad puffed away on a few Winstons.

Between Paladin and *Bonanza* I felt safe and full and dreamed of the day some family would be eating Snickers, drinking Cokes, and smoking while I entertained them on the "Kirstie show."

After my mother died, I was given three things of hers by my father: her sterling silver, her hand-etched crystal, and her rose-covered china.

I think of her every time I use it, and I use it a lot.

Especially when I invite the Queen of England for lunch.

Lillian in her prime, before she restricted her diet to Cokes and peanut M&Ms.

3

Cocaine and Dianetics

JANUARY 19TH—24TH, 2004

Got lots of Scientology sessions this week. Decided was not that old, especially if lived to be 112. Decided to write show for fat self. Decided it would take year to lose fat self, so better work fat, or self would starve. Ironic.

I did not do drugs in high school or college or while I was married the first time. No, I was very opposed to drug use. Hated the smell of pot and hated being around pot smokers. Too stupid, too slow, yes, well, too stoned.

Would never have thought of any drug in needle form. Hell, I used to bawl when I had to get a simple vaccination. So no, nothing would be shot into my pure veins. LSD was definitely out, too. Two of my girlfriends fried themselves on acid in college. One was basically left retarded, the other dead.

I hardly ever drank. Alcohol made me feel poisoned, and aside from piña coladas or sloe gin fizzes, I wasn't much interested.

But in 1976, after I left my husband for a wealthy, blue-eyed, Santa-smiled cowboy, I impetuously decided that one drug I might really like to try was cocaine.

Because I was always so high naturally to begin with, people would comment frequently, "Are you coked out?" "Are you high?" I'd say, "No, why?" And they'd say, "God, you have so much energy and you're so funny." I got the idea somewhere along the way that if I ever ran out of humor or energy, I should remember to give "blow" a chance.

While romancing cowboy Carl, fully madly in lust for the first time in my life, the opportunity arose. I was very shy in crowds, felt very inhibited. Never knew what to say or how to act. Anxiety attacks, one might call them, would regularly occur in a crowd.

Well, this particular crowd was called a wedding reception. A friend of cowboy Carl's had gotten married, and all had gathered at the Wichita Country Club for fun, dancing, and, oh yes, cocaine.

Cowboy asked me if I'd like to try some. I asked what cocaine did to people.

"Oh, it just makes you really extroverted, very high energy, very out there."

"Will I hallucinate?"

"Oh God, no, nothing like that, nothing at all like that, just this very 'aware' feeling and lots of energy and very chatty."

The chatty part sounded intriguing because I really didn't like talking to people at weddings or parties or receptions or funerals or, well, anyplace with a lot of people.

"Okay," I said, "let's give it a whirl."

I went into the bathroom with a friend of Carl's. She was a very good teacher. I was a very receptive pupil. She laid out two, 3-inch lines of white powder.

"Okay," she said, as she rolled up a $100 bill, "just put this up to your nose and sniff all the way down the line like this."

Up went the $100 bill to her nose, then sniffff.

"See?" she said. "Easy, you try."

Okay, sniffff. Yikes. Kind of harsh. Kind of smells like Novocain from the dentist's office.

"Good," she said. "Now rub the excess powder on your gums for an excellent freeze."

Oh God, yes sister, I need an excellent freeze . . . whatever that meant.

"Cool?" she asked.

Oh God, yes. Cool as a Popsicle, Sisterbelle.

"Cool," I answered.

We went back out into the raucous country club crowd. I felt no different.

Cowboy Carl spotted me.

"Did you do it?"

"Yeah."

"How'd you like it?"

"Yeah, it was cool."

"Cool," he said, "let's dance."

We began to dance. And about 2 minutes into a Pablo Cruise rendition, I began to feel as if I were going out of my body. It felt just like I felt when I was 8 and had been playing down by the creek in the deep, deep snow. I heard our dinner bell ring and began to run for home. Suddenly I fell into a snowdrift made by a hedge of 6-foot fir trees and the side of a hill. I fell in the drift between the trees, and the hill and the snow was well above my head. At first I panicked; I was sure I was going to die. Then I had this odd knowingness, this strange wisdom of what to do next.

I put my arms above my head and began to turn in a circle really fast, like a Roto-Rooter or a cartoon character boring a hole into the earth. I widened my arms and dropped my elbows down, making my arms look a little like a goalpost. Then I turned in circles again. I began to bend my knees while circling lower and lower and lower. Finally, I stopped.

Somehow I'd fashioned a perfect cylinder, and I do mean perfect. I sat and looked above me—the cylinder towered at least 4 feet over my head. I was not dead. I did not die of suffocation in the snowbank.

That's when I began to lift out of my body—not like people who astral project or astral walk—no, just left my body behind, and I was a few feet back or up or wherever the hell it was, but I was clearly not in my body.

The feeling of well-being was consuming. I'd only experienced it once before, at age 4, when I could briefly breathe under water like a fish. I couldn't explain that either, but I could breathe underwater like a fish until my mother told me I couldn't.

I felt so relaxed and peaceful and safe. I'll never forget the ecstasy of those 5 minutes. I felt as though I could sit there until the end of time. I felt there was no time. I wanted this feeling forever. I felt like no one would ever leave me. And that's exactly how I felt again in 1975 on that dance floor at the Wichita Country Club.

I immediately made a decision and then a vow.

"I will snort cocaine every day for the rest of my life."

No kidding, no shit, Kirstie Lou was dead serious.

"Every day for the rest of my life."

And thus, a cocaine addict was born. Yes, hatched actually, like some alien pod girl crawling out of her introverted chicken shell.

Here I am, Wichita, hear me roar! I may have been nothing, but now I'm a coke whore!

Transformations this abrupt are usually seen only in movies, and convictions this extreme seen only in the Green Berets.

And so it went for about 3 years. You could always recognize Kirstie Lou by the gritting teeth and permanent white powder outline of her nostrils. Not too many people noticed, unfortunately. "Most" thought me no more nutty than usual. Besides, "most" that I hung out with had powdered nostrils also.

Cowboy Carl and I began to decorate our love nest up there in College Hill Park. Carl took me to a well-known design company, which also happened to be the biggest florist in Wichita. Carl and I sat with the owner and selected *the* most gorgeous furniture, fabrics, wall coverings—just stunning.

The design owner, Dean, said to me, "You are a very talented interior designer." I thanked Dean.

He said, "You should come and work for me."

With the false confidence of the cocaine surging through my veins, I accepted. "When would you like me to start, Mr. Dean?"

"How about Monday morning?"

"I'll be there."

Just like that, pod girl had been given the Doris-day pillow talk opportunity of a lifetime. Just like that. Just like that.

On Monday I showed up for duty, un-stoned. I was primarily a weekend cokehead, although the weekends now stretched from Thursday until Sunday.

Dean gave me my first client. A very rich bachelor who owned a huge plumbing company in Wichita.

"Vincent will really like you. He's a little difficult, but he likes the ladies and you two will hit it off, I'm sure."

Off to Vincent's house I drove. When I pulled into Vincent's driveway, I saw three Mercedes Benzs, one Bentley, and a Shelby Cobra. Vincent was doing well in the plumbing business, that's for sure.

Vincent greeted me at his door, middle of the day. Vincent's house was very dark and Vincent wore sunglasses inside the house.

He welcomed me in, asked me to take a seat, and promptly shoved a 4-by-4 silver box in front of my face.

"Do you like blow?" he asked.

"Yes, Vincent, I like blow."

"Then you're the designer for me."

And such was my interior design relationship with Vincent. Every time I took fabrics or furniture to his house, I got high.

Soon my weekend extended from Wednesday through Sunday.

Most of my clients were straight, not druggies at all. Straight, well-monied, conservative, Wichita highbrows. Vincent introduced me to all his friends, of course. Most of them drug dealers. My new, well-salaried design position now afforded me all the snow I could blow. And, of course, Cowboy Carl purchased a lot of the white stuff, too, and was always very generous with it.

I remember a night Cowboy and I laid a couple of ounces of cocaine out on the glass dining room table. It made a line 6 feet long and ½ inch wide. Looked more like a trench than a line, actually. Thousands of dollars worth of powder lay there just waiting for the eager coke-snorting guests we'd invited to stop by.

Within minutes, the swarmlike "best friends" had converged on the cocaine highway and poof, literally poof, it was all breathed up and all spreading like a hideous virus through all our capillaries and veins and bloodstreams.

Yum yum. Yee ha! What a scrumptious life we were all leading.

Soon followed hundreds of yummy nights like this one—each causing pod girl to get thinner and thinner and thinner until pod girl weighed about 110 pounds with huge, green eyes and chronically dilated pupils.

I began taking massive amounts of vitamins to counter the excellent powder. I began to keep a journal. Not much else to do at 5:00 A.M. when the rest of the world is sleeping or rising for a new day. This journal was so profound. All my most inner, psychotic, paranoid thoughts recorded therein.

I was fabulous, cocaine fabulous.

Cowboy Carl would buy me anything I wanted, and more. Everybody loved me, just everybody. Sure, I was the one with the drugs, but that's not why they loved me. It was because I was no longer Kirstie Lou, divorcée, introverted, shy girl.

No, now I was Kirstie Fabulous. Snow queen of College Hill Park. I was fabulous.

And so it went, until one fabulous day in 1978, when Kirstie Fabulous went fabulously insane.

Cowboy Carl had proposed to me and I'd accepted. I had a huge rock on my left hand, but I hadn't slept in several days. My size two jeans were baggy, and the Valiums I was now popping in order not to have anxiety attacks were no longer working. I'd not done any cocaine for about 10 days, and yet I was still anxious and still going quite mad.

I decided to head out into the country to stay with my friends, Carmen and Dick. Get away from all the people and drug dealers and drug friends and parties and glass dining room tables and Fleetwood Mac concerts.

But before I went to the country, I needed to stop by my house and pick up a few things to wear, toothbrush, pajamas. I pulled in the driveway, got out of the car, and went into the kitchen, where I sat down for a little rest.

Some friends, a family from down the street, came into my kitchen. I began to laugh.

"What are you guys doing here?"

They laughed, too.

"God, Kirstie, you're funny. What are we doing here? We live here."

I laughed some more, then I realized Snow Queen pod girl was in the wrong house. That's right, I was sitting in my neighbor friend's house, a block away from my own. I sloughed it off, laughed about it.

"Duh!" I said, "I was just kidding!"

They thought I was, too. Their only other choice would have been: lunatic.

I stayed at Dick and Carmen's house for 5 days. So paranoid and crazy that I couldn't really be anywhere, comfortably. I pitched a tent on their living room floor and stayed mostly inside it eating Beenie Weenies and watching reruns of *Leave It to Beaver*. Each time I'd pop out of the tent I'd get confused and anxious, so back in I'd pop.

After days of this hand-wringing ordeal, a fellow cocaine-using, drug-addicted, med school friend of mine came to my rescue with a bottle of Valium—to help calm me down.

Down is a very good way to describe Fabulous Kirstie. I knew for a fact that I was certifiable. People had always said, "Oh Kirstie, you're crazy." And, by crazy, they meant fun, funny.

But I knew I was in serious trouble and that this was no longer funny. I was dying spiritually. I was down for the count. What was it Ernest Hemingway said after his shock therapy, right before he committed suicide, " . . . It was a brilliant cure, but we lost the patient." That's what I could feel happening.

I was disappearing, and this whole conglomeration of neurosis and psychosis and paranoia, a mental gobbledygook, was taking over. I was drowning in a mire of unidentifiable identities, none of my own. I could feel the abyss but inches away.

I took the Valiums and they relieved the terrible anxiety.

I spent that night on a real bed at Dick and Carmen's and left with Dr. Drug Addict the next morning, heading back to Carl's. I lived on Valium for the next 2 weeks, until Cowboy Carl had an old friend come to visit us. I was jealous of the California friend. She was beautiful and charming and rich and funny and well . . . perfect. I got wind from my next-door neighbor that "California" was a Scientologist.

All I knew about Scientology is that I once saw a Scientology center in Los Angeles and the parking lot was full of snazzy cars. So at least I knew that Scientologists must like snazzy cars.

One night, after Cowboy Carl went to sleep and left me alone to converse with "California," I got up the nerve to ask her a question.

"Can Scientology help someone get rid of the urge to do stupid things like drugs?"

She answered yes.

I asked my last question, "Can Scientology help a person get over anxiety attacks?"

Again, she said yes.

"California" went back to California on Tuesday. The following

Monday I received a book in the mail. I had stopped taking Valium, but had done a couple of grams of cocaine. I was feeling only moderately insane, so I thought it might be time to roll out the barrels again, so to speak.

The book was *Dianetics*, which translates to "what the soul is doing to the body." This definition was of interest to me. No doubt my soul was wreaking havoc on my body. My soul was sick, my soul was fading out.

I sat on a white chaise lounge in a white room with white carpets and a white tile sunken tub—I'd designed this room for Cowboy Carl. I drank cherry limeade, snorted cocaine off a perfume mirror, and began to read *Dianetics: The Modern Science of Mental Health*, first published in 1950.

This was my routine for 4 days. Cherry limeade, cocaine, and *Dianetics*. On the 5th day, I completed the book and decided that Dianetics was either the biggest scam in the universe, or it would lead me out of my self-created hell. I informed Cowboy Carl I would be leaving him in 30 days to move to California to check out Dianetics and Scientology and find out for myself.

I quit my job with Dean. I announced what I was doing to my family. I began to pack my things for the move to California. I knew two people in California, Sarah Campbell, a childhood friend who was married to Glenn Campbell, and one other girl I knew vaguely, Polly. I snorted massive amounts of cocaine to get up the nerve to leave my home of 28 years.

A friend drove with me to California. What is normally a 3-day drive took us 26 days, as we scored cocaine all over the United States. We zigzagged up, over, back, and forward until we finally arrived in Los Angeles.

I snorted the last of my cocaine on a Sunday night and went to the Scientology center in Sherman Oaks on Monday. Miraculously, and I do mean miraculously, I had one Scientology session and never did cocaine again. Not a single speck.

And even more miraculously, I have never, since that day, had a single fleeting urge to partake in the snowy white powder. I rebuilt my life, made amends to all I'd harmed while on drugs, and 2 years later starred in my first movie. I never had another anxiety attack, and I've never taken any other drugs.

I'm eternally grateful to "California" for being there when I needed someone so desperately. I've made up for the damage I caused by serving as the international spokesperson for Narconon for the last 18 years, and helping millions to become educated about drugs, and thousands of others to get off drugs.

I am glad I read *Dianetics*. It was the first time it literally saved my ass, not to mention my life.

Yikes! Here's my screen test for "Dead Woman Walking."
Me? High? What was the clue? 1978.

I'm pretty and skinny and so very happy—or am I dead?
I always get those two confused . . .

Lies, a Trilogy

Call Me Sandy

January 28th, 2004

IRS paid off. Made policy to pay more attention to taxes. Made policy to not accidentally spend tax "set-asides." Made policy to get accurate definition of "tax set-asides." Made policy to seek out movie for fat leading lady.

February 14th, 2004

Valentine's Day. Realize have not had valentine in 4 years. Realize have not had sex in 4 years also. Decide not to have sex for 1 more year. Fat sex would be no good. Fat sex would be ass. Remembered that many times skinny sex was ass, too. Yes, skinny sex had led me down road to blindness many times. So, no fat sex, no skinny sex, no sex period. Like Buddhist monk in training. No sex until learned lesson that sex is not love. Sex is not marriage. Lust is not love. Sex and lust not pre-req for "man of dreams." Also, moment of orgasm not good time to decide man on top of me is "man of dreams." Decide good idea to know man on top of me having sex and orgasms really, really well before deeming him "man of dreams," as violation of policy has potential of becoming "man of nightmares."

FEBRUARY 20TH, 2004

Lied to friend. Said could not go to fancy Hollywood party with her because had children and no sitter. Truth: Did not go to fancy Hollywood party because fat and mortified might see Johnny Depp, Keanu Reeves, Kid Rock, or realtor guy from Under the Tuscan Sun. *Said had small sinus infection.*

MARCH 6TH, 2004

Lied to children about not taking them to premiere screening of big Disney movie. Said now had serious, life-threatening sinus infection. Truth: Had serious life-threatening phobia of photos being taken at screening and enormous butt spread across new tabloid. Re-made decision from past, stop lying, especially to children.

When I was young, I used to lie about the most casual things. Not about "did I break this or did I take that"—no, I lied about things that were at the very core of my being. Such as my name, Kirstie—weird name—no one ever pronounced it correctly.

People always said Christy or Kirsty or Kristen or Curtsy or Christa, etc. Even my own grandmother Maud spelled it wrong her entire life. My name at one point was almost Allison. Hmmm, Allison Alley—not good. And at another point, after both of my grandmothers in combination—Maudanna—Maud for Maud, and Anna for Annabelle. Maudanna is without a doubt the ugliest name I've ever heard, so at least Kirstie was better than that. But still, jeez, no one could pronounce it except for very small children, who got it when I would say, "It's Kirstie, like thirsty—Kirstie." They listened to what I was saying and always said it correctly from then on out. But to adults, I'd say, "It's Kirstie, like thirsty, Kirstie," and they'd say, "Yeah right, Christy, yeah right, Curtsy."

I thought then what I later learned was very true: adults rarely really listen to children. They are much too busy ordering them about or lecturing them or placating them with a sort of out-to-lunch, glib, half-assed acknowledgment like, "yes, yes, I see" when of course, they don't see anything. They are, in truth, certifiably blind.

The name Kirstie was given to me, as the story goes, because I looked slightly like Loretta Young at birth and Loretta Young once played a nun named "Kirstie" in an episode of the *Loretta Young Show*.

But why, I wondered, not just Loretta? Easy enough to pronounce and a lovely name. And did I look like a nun at birth, or like Loretta herself? But, somehow, in my parents' minds, Kirstie was the correct tag for their second girl child.

Anyhoo, it was about age 6 that I began calling myself Sandy whenever I had the chance in private moments, like at the YMCA swimming pool, at acrobat class when someone new enrolled, or at Sheplers, a famous western store in Wichita, Kansas.

I just couldn't bear any more of the bastardizations of my already ridiculous name. And then, of course, along with my new "handle" came my new stories. Too many to recount, but the Sheplers one went like this.

Sheplers used to have these sawhorse things that the saddles were displayed on. I was atop one of these steeds when a woman said, "Hi, what's your name?"

What do you think, Dumbbell? My name is Sandy, fool, Sandy.

Of course I really just said, "Sandy."

"Sandy. Oh, Sandy is a pretty name and it suits you to a T. Sandy, where do you live?"

Another stupid question from the nosey bitch.

"We live on a huge ranch in western Kansas." Hmmm. I'd heard "western Kansas" from my dad, who had a brother who lived in "western Kansas," and it didn't seem like a big ranch, a big western ranch, would be in "southern" Kansas, now did it?

"Oh really, how exciting. How many acres?"

"Thousands!"

"Oh Sandy, how thrilling for you, and do you have horses on your ranch?"

"Hundreds."

"Hundreds? Oh my, what a wonderful life you must lead."

Yes, snoopy, it is a wonderful life, albeit it's only in my mind, it is one of the most wonderful lives anyone could ever live. I ride in rodeos and I personally have 10 horses, and my father is a bachelor just like Brian Keith in *The Parent Trap*, and we have a huge pond for swimming. And I have monkeys and a llama and a zebra.

Lions and tigers and bears, oh my! My life became glorious, jubilant, as I informed Snoop Dog about the holdings of my made-up family. When she asked about my mother, who was standing across the store buying red cowboy boots for my brother, I said, as though it caused me deep sadness, "Divorced. She left him."

I could pretty much tell with all our land and horses and ponds and monkeys and all that, this woman was ready to move to "western Kansas" with my fictional clan and marry dear ole deserted dad.

About 30 minutes later, as my mother and brother and I were leaving Sheplers, the woman hollered, "Goodbye, Sandy! It was great to meet you."

My mother said, "Sandy? Why would she call you Sandy?"

"Just another person who can't pronounce Kirstie, I guess."

Why would I want to change my identity: I clearly had it all goin' on!

“Sandy,” age 26. Graduated to a real horse. Is that Brian Keith I see behind that tree?

5

What Does Baby Want?

March 15th, 2004

Completed creating concept for Fat Actress, *new series about girl with fat ass struggling in Hollywood with work, men, age, weight, sex, food, bills, friends, taxes, family, and love.*

Hmm, "Fat Actress" apparently could be girl with or without fat ass, with or without being actress.

Hmm . . . apparently, "Fat Actress" is universal metaphor for "women."

March 17th, 2004

Met with Brenda Hampton, creator/producer of TV series Seventh Heaven. *Good fit for* Fat Actress. *Antithesis of* Seventh Heaven.

Liked her a lot. Good match—understands big-bottomed girls, although has tiny-bottom self.

Excited to partner with tiny-bottomed Brenda Hampton.

MARCH 24TH, 2004

Had appointment with big hotshots at Showtime to pitch giant-bottomed actress show. Decide to wash hair and *put on makeup. Went to big Showtime meeting with clean hair, makeup, and high heels. Also wore black jacket to camouflage gigantic posterior. Big shots laughed and laughed. (At pitch, not posterior.)*

Bought Fat Actress *in the room.*

Rewarded self with big lunch at Mr. Chows and two dips of Daiquiri Ice at Baskin-Robbins. Dreamed of wild sex with Ben Affleck—was skinny in dream. (Me, not him.)

APRIL 1ST, 2004

Called close friends nationwide and told them had sex previous night with big Hollywood actor. None of them were fooled.

Lost 2 pounds running like fool on treadmill for 1½ hours, wondering why friends didn't believe big Hollywood April fool's story. Wondering if really big Hollywood actress would ever have sex again with even really small Hollywood B-movie actor, or worse, Hollywood soap opera actor, or even worse, industrial film actor, or tragically, Broadway musical comedy actor.

I remember this date I had once in the early eighties.

He and I zigzagged flirtatiously, winding in and out of each other on a well-known canyon road in LA. He was on a Harley-Davidson. I was in a $16,000 stereo system disguised as a convertible Toyota Celica. He motioned for me to follow him—something I was not inclined to do, but it was springtime, my top was down (no pun intended), and after all, he was an actor I'd seen before. So I answered his beckoning and followed him.

He spent the afternoon boxing a friend of his, and I was the audience. Very macho stuff that boxing, and admittedly, it was sexy watching two guys beat the hell out of each other.

He asked me out for the coveted Saturday night time slot—reserved only for the few, the proud, the privileged.

Over the course of the evening, it became quite clear that he was somewhat of an idiot, and that the boxing had been the high point of our tryst. He drove me home, and to be polite (the downfall of my personality), I agreed it would be fine for him to come inside for a late-night coffee.

Of course, I don't drink coffee, didn't know how to make it, and really wanted to get rid of the guy—but it did sound like the civil, adult thing to do. After I pretended to drink the coffee, he made a proposal.

"I want to make love to you."

Now, all of my friends had recently told me, "God Kirstie, you don't have to marry a guy just because you sleep with him." Now that sounds like very hip, single girl advice, doesn't it? Actually, I aspired to be the kind of girl who could participate in lovely, casual sex and then just move on to the next casual sexer. So in this 5-second period of time I made my decision.

"No, I don't think that's a good idea . . . we've only just met and as fun as this date was, I think the timing is not right."

Man, that sounded smooth! I was shocked that this came out so, well, experienced! And ethical!

But then an odd thing happened—something I'd really never seen before. The actor began to weep. Great big crocodile tears.

"Wow. I just feel so close to you. I just . . . well . . . I know it's corny, but I'm falling in love with you."

Corny? Hell, no! Not for me. Love—love, did he say? Well, even though I think he's a complete idiot, "love" might be at stake here—love, marriage, children, ding dong! I might be passing up my future Mr. Actor!

"All right, then. I didn't know that's how you really felt."

He took my hand and walked me up the badly carpeted chocolate brown steps to my bedroom. He undressed me. I knew my body rocked, so I proudly stood there like the model slash goddess slash stunner I thought I was.

Then it was my turn. I took off his shirt to a very previously choreographed "You can ring my bell." I unbuckled his very groovy biker belt and let the pants drop dramatically to the floor. I slid ever so stealthily, like an Abyssinian cat between the T.J. Maxx sateen sheets. He equally as professionally slid in beside me—nose to nose, eyes to eyes. My hands (as they say in romance novels) began to read his body.

Then a very strange thing happened—while I was reading his body, I realized he had no hair on his chest. Or his arms or his legs, actually.

No, he wasn't a chick—not that that didn't cross my mind.

I began to sweat. The anxiety began to sweep me away.

Shut up, shut up, Kirstie—so what if he's hairless, so what? Stop only thinking about the physical. Get into it for God's sake!

Again, I was a pro.

I slipped my hand ever so gently down his throat, across his barren chest and nonexistent treasure trail onto . . . what could best be described as a small child's thumb. Or, should I say, a small child's erect thumb.

Panic and terror blasted through me in waves. I'd read about this with Jean Harlow and her husband who committed suicide because of his miniature equipment. I didn't want the boy to kill himself . . . or did I? At one moment it seemed that one of us surely would after this encounter, and I was certainly too young to die. Thoughts I'd never had raced through my head.

Is this for real? Is this guy a chick with a dick? Does this moron not know he has the world's smallest Johnson—by Guinness standards? Would he not think it appropriate to announce beforehand,

"Hey, my penis is the size of a cheap eraser, so before we embark I'd like you to have the opportunity to decide whether or not to proceed?"

But the most prevalent thought was, *How in the hell am I going to get off with a baby cock like this?*

I calmed myself before taking responsibility. I knew I'd gotten myself into this mess. And hadn't I heard on *Sixty Minutes* that many serial killers had no hair and little peckers?

Oh my, back to the responsibility, but wait, he was beginning to speak.

Maybe he would explain that perhaps he'd had polio in the penis as a child, or maybe he would talk about his time in 'Nam and how Agent Orange had caused all of his hair to fall out and his watson to shrink from its original size to that of a toddler's.

Instead he said, with bold virility, "What does baby want?"

Did I hear that right?

Yes, I did, because he repeated it with ever more masculine commitment, "What does baby want? Tell Daddy what baby wants."

It was all I could do not to scream—baby wants a cock! Jesus, it doesn't have to be a porn cock but come on, asshole, Baby wants a fucking *real,* at least average-sized one!

Instead . . . I kept thinking of poor Jean Harlow's husband—the shame and degradation and, of course, the suicide. His last actual fuck, as I personally believe suicides are, in fact the committer's final, grandiose "fuck you!" Nevertheless, I did always worry about penile suicide prospects. It haunted me for years actually. Jean Harlow's sad, tiny-tallywacker'd suicidal husband.

I said casually, as if I'd experienced this kind of thing hundreds of times in my work as a prostitute . . . "this is what baby wants" . . . I put my peace sign–giving fingers between my legs. I deduced it was the only possible hope to get this guy off and out of my house.

He complimented this ingenious idea.

"Oh baby, you've been around," he said.

Of course. In my line of work, you need to know all the tricks of the trade—after all—you never know when your pimp might set you up with a gentleman who makes a preschooler's rod look like John Holmes'.

After he finished fucking the peace sign and I finished faking the most pathetic orgasm to date, even by faker standards, he rolled off me in bliss.

"Damn baby, damn that was good!"

Of course it was, buddy boy, but just remember if it hadn't been for Mr. sad, dead, suicidal Harlow and his tragic farewell, you, your underdeveloped appendage, and overdeveloped ego would never have come close to heaven's gate. Peace sign or no peace sign.

Left: Baby wants to be of service.

Top right: Baby wants Rock Hudson to call. Oh my—I guess he has!

Bottom right: Baby wants great Grandma to play racket ball . . . Baby's bored.

6

LIES, A TRILOGY

THE SWING

APRIL 7TH, 2004

Went to best friend John Travolta's 50th birthday party in Mexico. Went on private plane—was fattest girl on plane, then at party. Was very introverted around other thin stars. Had not smoked in 5 years, but when offered a smoke by prince from Jordan, and after three shots of tequila, decided to partake. Did not feel so fat when was drinking tequila and smoking cigarettes. Wondered why hadn't married John Travolta . . .

APRIL 9TH, 2004

Did not feel good today. Felt hungover and addicted to cigarettes. Now have to lose weight and *quit smoking. Decide no more Hollywood par-*

ties until thin and have stopped smoking, and decide no more regrets about John and embarrassed thoughts about why hadn't married him. Why hadn't married John always rears ludicrous head when a.) have had any alcohol, b.) see him dance, or c.) watch reruns of Urban Cowboy.

John is big one who got away. That's *why am fat,* that *is big mystery, that is ruin of life and demise of career. That's why get hives when nervous, and why feet hurt when exercising—why eating cakes and pies and fudge and doughnuts and fried chicken and Cheetos. Why have been celibate for 4 years. Because of John, John, Johnny boy Travolta!!!*

APRIL 10TH, 2004

Made up big lie about John Travolta in journal yesterday. Deciding whether to revise submission or let stand. Decide to let stand.

Lying began to really start working for me at around 4½. This sort-of-cute bachelor type moved in next door to us on Estelle Street. The first house I'd lived in, thus my porn name: Moto Estelle. Moto, my first dog, Estelle, my first street.

Anyway, this very mildly handsome guy, probably in his early twenties, would not pay quite enough attention to me for my liking.

At age 4½, I thought I was Bridget Bardot. Seriously, I thought I was an extraordinary beauty—movie star beautiful. This notion truly came from Mars, as I was not stunning or much of anything out of the ordinary. But I had no doubts that when men laid eyes on me, especially men from about 18 to 25, their heads would spin off their axes and they would froth at the mouth.

When I saw movie magazines and glamour shots of the most

beautiful starlets in Hollywood, I would sort of scoff at them thinking—knowing—I was far superior in beauty and talent than they. Perhaps last lifetime I was "they." Perhaps I hadn't quite come to grips that I was in a new body at a new time and that I was 4½ years old.

Anyhoo, the man next door, although not handsome enough for me by my Hollywood standards, was, however, a pushover, and this, plus a couple of doozies I'd told him, meant I had him in my hip pocket.

His name was Donny. Donny was swinging me on our swing set the day after he moved in. He'd been doing this for about 20 minutes, when he announced that he had to go back in his house and get some work done.

"Can't you swing me just a little longer?"

"No, honey," he said, "but I'm sure your dad will swing you when he comes home."

"Daddy? Daddy, did you say?"

I feigned a slight pout, that starlet pout that drives perverts and poets mad, as I said, "I don't have a daddy!"

Zip! This caught his "I'm gonna go in the house and do some work" ass by surprise.

"You don't have a daddy?"

"No, sir." ("Sir" was something I'd heard Miss Kitty say on *Gunsmoke.*)

"No sir, my daddy is dead. He got killed in the war."

His face turned ashen as I reeled him in.

"The war, huh?"

"Yes sir, the war."

"Uh, er, okay, well, I'll swing you for your daddy, honey, I sure will."

This was perhaps my greatest performance to date. Oscar material, really, for such a young ingénue. Donny swing, swang, swung me until it began to get dark. That's the longest anyone ever swing, swang, swung me.

I was in Nirvana, eyes half closed, pumping my legs like a little hooker when I heard . . .

"Hey, Kirstie Lou, it's time for dinner."

My half-closed eyes sprung open like mousetraps! Yikes, my dad—yikes!

My dad introduced himself, saying, "Hi, I'm Robert." And Donny said, "Hi, I'm Donny" and they both shook hands.

My heart pounded like Ricky Ricardo's bongos. Then the dreaded words no starlet would ever want to hear:

"I'm just swinging Kirstie because her dad died in the war and she doesn't really have anyone to swing her anymore."

Dad, close your ears, don't listen, the guy is a pathological liar. He's cuckoo, he's a lunatic. He just broke out of the nuthouse. Dad, he's a blithering shock victim who knows not what he says.

My dad looked at me like a heat-seaking missile in slow motion, and when he spoke, his voice was altered like the monster from the Black Lagoon.

"Oh really? Where did you hear that? I'm Kirstie's dad."

I'm Kirstie's dad? Why did my father have to say such stupid shit all the time? I'm Kirstie's dad? Why didn't he just say I'm Adolph Hitler or Mussolini but no, I'm Kirstie's dad? What an ass. God, fathers can be such dicks sometimes.

I quietly bestowed Donny boy with my best Scarlett O'Hara fluttering, flirty butterfly eyes, *Oh God, oh please, Donny boy, don't betray me, don't throw me to the dogs.*

"Oh, I just heard that from someone down the street, must be the wrong kid."

God, I love you, Donny. Boy, you may not be handsome, like Clark Gable, but I swear to God I'll give you a job in my next film.

As my dad walked me back inside the house, he said, "You know, Kirstie Lou, it's a lot easier to tell the truth than to lie. It makes life a lot simpler."

This taught me a great lesson, and I had no doubt in my mind after I heard those words that my father was . . . a complete moron without the faintest idea of how to operate in Tinseltown—poor, poor, poor, silly misguided daddy.

Top: This is not a Pekignese. This is a black panther, believe me.

Bottom: I don't look like a pathological liar, do I?

My father—taken two years after he was killed in the Korean War . . . uh-oh!

LIES, A TRILOGY

ANNABELLE'S FABULOUS TRAVELING RAT SHOW

APRIL 15TH, 2004

Celebrated having already paid big IRS taxes. Celebrated with sausage gravy and biscuits for breakfast, Arby's for lunch, and big Italian dinner from Farfalla. Continue celebration for next 5 days, eating way across Hollywood into Malibu.

APRIL 20TH, 2004

Showtime says want Fat Actress *but can't give definitive "pick up" until June. Get angry and throw computer on floor. After purchasing new*

MacTitanium, decide to put attention on other fat roles. Decide to do documentary on self being fat and self getting back to self. Decide to get honest and straight with self. No more lies to self. Self sick of lies. Have to eat big cake to get over self-sickness.

A good rule of thumb is that when you are not getting enough attention or when your life is not very interesting . . . just lie about it. Lying has so many unknown benefits really. Sure, some people lie to get out of jams or for criminal reasons, but the best lies, the most useful ones, pertain to creating a more full and interesting life for yourself.

These are the lies that can easily be justified, because they actually provide pleasure and excitement to others who live dull, boring lives also. It somehow gives them hope, so in these instances I believe lying is both a social endeavor and an artistic endeavor, to be practiced freely. Or at least that's the way I used to feel, and what used to be my philosophy, until the first grade when I was shown that the fine art of lying could turn on you and result in the most humiliating travesty of a young life.

This was the year I decided to stop lying forever—okay, that's a lie.

This was the year I decided to stop lying about silly, irrelevant, insignificant things—another lie.

All right, this was the year I decided to stop lying when the odds were that my parents would get wind of the lie and punish me severely—there we go, that's the truth! Whew!

There were very interesting children in my first grade class. One kid, Kip, now and then brought a flask of bourbon to school and sipped it on the monkey bars at recess. Then there was Larry, who I had crushes on, off and on until the seventh grade, whose mother only had one arm. Then there was Linda, whose brother had been run over by her father and dragged down the street several hundred yards.

By comparison I lived a flat, boring existence.

Show-and-tell was the place where "what kids were made of" was revealed. Oh sure, there were the kids with dog pictures: "This is our dog Mitsy. Yes, Mitsy bit the postman and then had to be put down."

Or, "Here is a medal my grandfather got in World War II. He got shrapnel in his eye and is blind."

Or, "Here is the box of kittens my cat Trixy had 2 weeks ago. Mama says not to touch them because your cooties could give them distemper and kill them."

Every week pretty interesting stuff being shown and told. But what was I supposed to show or tell?

Here's my dog Lady, we've had her for 12 years, or here's a picture of my brother Craig—who is not particularly of interest since he goes to the same school and you can see him walking with me any day of the week.

I had a normal family, no missing limbs, no alcoholism . . . no kittens. We were all allergic to cats, so no kittens, except for the cat I brought home on Halloween that had been spray painted green, and that I kept locked in the garage and fed bacon to twice a day—until my mother found him and gave him away and replaced him with a new, full-blooded Siamese cat. Not a stray, a Siamese cat that ended up giving me, my sister, my brother, my two cousins, and the kid across the street ringworm. No, sir. Cats were no good for our family.

My life was uneventful, without merit—a complete reflection

of the banalness of me. I had nothing for show-and-tell, nothing at all, nothing.

But I wanted something to tell, I really did, and so on one Friday at 2:30 in the afternoon, the show-and-tell slot, I stood before the first grade class of the South Hillside School and shared a piece of my exciting life.

"My grandmother, Annabelle, raises white rats. You might not know this, but rats are very, very smart. My grandmother has taught her rats to come and fetch and to dance. She dresses them in little homemade clothes that she and her quilting club make. They have hats and skirts and pants and dresses and even tiny little rat shoes.

"My grandmother has taken her rats all over the world so people can see their act. I would have had her come here with them today, but presently she is in Switzerland with them. Well, that's it. I know you'd really like to see the rats. Maybe next year. Maybe around Christmas, when Grandma dresses them like Santa and his reindeer—their reindeer suits are swell—I'll bring them in. Thank you."

I don't think I have, to this day, felt what that moment felt like. A fixed attention on me, an awe of what I was saying. A complete command of the entire first grade class, including Miss Boulby, who looked nothing short of astonished. All this time she'd had pure gold in her classroom, a student whose grandmother had a road show of traveling costumed dancing rats. Right under her nose was this vast wealth of interest and worldliness.

I felt a little sorry for the next kid up for show-and-tell. Her name was Karen B. (because we had five Karens in the class).

Karen B. brought a lame nurse's hat that her mother had worn when she was saving soldiers' lives in Korea—poor dumb Karen B.—and her lame nurse's hat.

Children treated me differently from there on out—more respect, more reverence. I became the opinion leader of the class. I was on cloud nine, hell, cloud ten. And all because of nine tiny rodents.

Months later, my mother and father returned from "conferences" at South Hillside School. You know, a sort of "verbal" report card. I was having lunch—Campbell's chicken rice soup, my favorite.

My dad said, "Kirstie Lou, have you been fibbing at school?"

Fibbing? Fibbing? Define fibbing exactly—fibbing, oh god, no Daddy Dearest, whatever do you mean?

"No."

"Miss Boulby just asked me, 'Now, is it your mother or your wife's mother who has the little white dancing rats?'"

Oh shit, oh shit, shit, shit.

"Hmm, hmm."

"Kirstie Lou? Did you tell a fib to Miss Boulby and the class about your grandmother raising white rats?"

Fib? How can I possibly answer the question if you continue to use words I do not understand?

There was really nowhere to turn, no cover. My cover was blown, blown, blown.

Now, you would think that what was really important to me would be my impending punishment, but in fact it was not.

"So, she believed the story?" I asked.

"Yes, Kirstie Lou, she believed the story."

This is the moment when I decided to become an actress. If a

40-year-old woman believed a whopper like that, hook, line, and sinker, well, then I was a pretty damn good storyteller.

Yes, I shall become a world-renowned actress and tell story upon story.

Daddy Dearest was not finished with Kirstie Lou, the fibber, however.

"You told your whole class this fib too, didn't you?"

Fib, fib? Where in the hell did he get this word. Why doesn't he just come out and say it—lie, lie, lie! Did you lie?

"Yes, I did Daddy."

"I see, okay, here's what we're going to do."

Uh oh, *we're*. When parents include themselves in "we're," you know you're up shit's creek. This collective decision that "they" have just made independently of you. Oh shit, all hell was about to break loose. Were *we* going to spank me? Or were *we* going to ground me? What exactly were *we* going to do to me?

"We're going to go over to the school now, and you're going to tell Miss Boulby and the class that you were fibbing, and that your grandmother doesn't raise rats or dress them up or teach them to dance and tour the world in a rat equivalent of the Moulin Rouge."

He's got to be kidding—I told this "fib" months ago. They probably don't even remember it.

"No Daddy, please," I began to whimper and beg. "No Daddy, please don't make me do that, please."

"Kirstie Lou, you need to learn that fibbing is not the way to live. Hell, I was a big ole liar until I was 14, and I realized it was a lot harder to lie than to tell the truth. This is for your own good. Let's go, Kirstie Lou."

A million tears were shed in the following 15 minutes as Daddy dragged me, literally, as my arms were wrapped around his legs, down the block to South Hillside School. Waves of grief erupted from me—"Please Daddy, no! Please Daddy nooooooooooo! I'll do anything Daddy, I'll never fib again, I swear to God, Daddy, pleeeease."

At the entrance of the school Daddy said, "Pull yourself together Kirstie Lou, they will not hate you, they will understand."

Did he really think I was worried about hate or understanding? For Christ's sake, Robert Deal Alley, I'm worried about saving face here! I'm worried about being just another average run-of-the-mill, boring kid here at South Hillside School. I'm worried that my status will be crushed as the queen of interesting grandparents, and that any future lies I tell my class will be met with skepticism and doubt.

You are about to destroy me, Robert Alley, you are about to turn me into every other lackluster, mediocre student in America!

"Hi, Miss Boulby. Hi class. Kirstie has something she'd like to tell you."

One thousand pounds of grief and despair pushed down on my body.

"I . . . I . . . I fibbed about my grandmother with the rats . . ."

There, I said it! There, burn me! Shun me! Shackle me!

I learned something funny about children that day.

They all looked at me like, yeah, so, we knew you were lying, but who cares, it was a good story, very entertaining. Not a flinch, they just resumed coloring in their coloring books.

I guess that only Miss Boulby had believed me. Perhaps because her life was also so desperately boring that she clung to the hope that someone would leave Wichita, Kansas, and South Hillside School and travel around the world with their amazing rat show.

She looked sad; she still wished it had been true. My dad

was wrong to have had me apologizing, and my dad usually was not wrong. But in this case, what good did it serve? The story was not delivered with malice. It was not intended to harm.

And wouldn't everyone have been much better off left with the impression that somewhere, high on a mountaintop in Switzerland, rats, dressed in top hats and tails, were dancing and swaying to the gentle rhythm of the Vienna waltz?

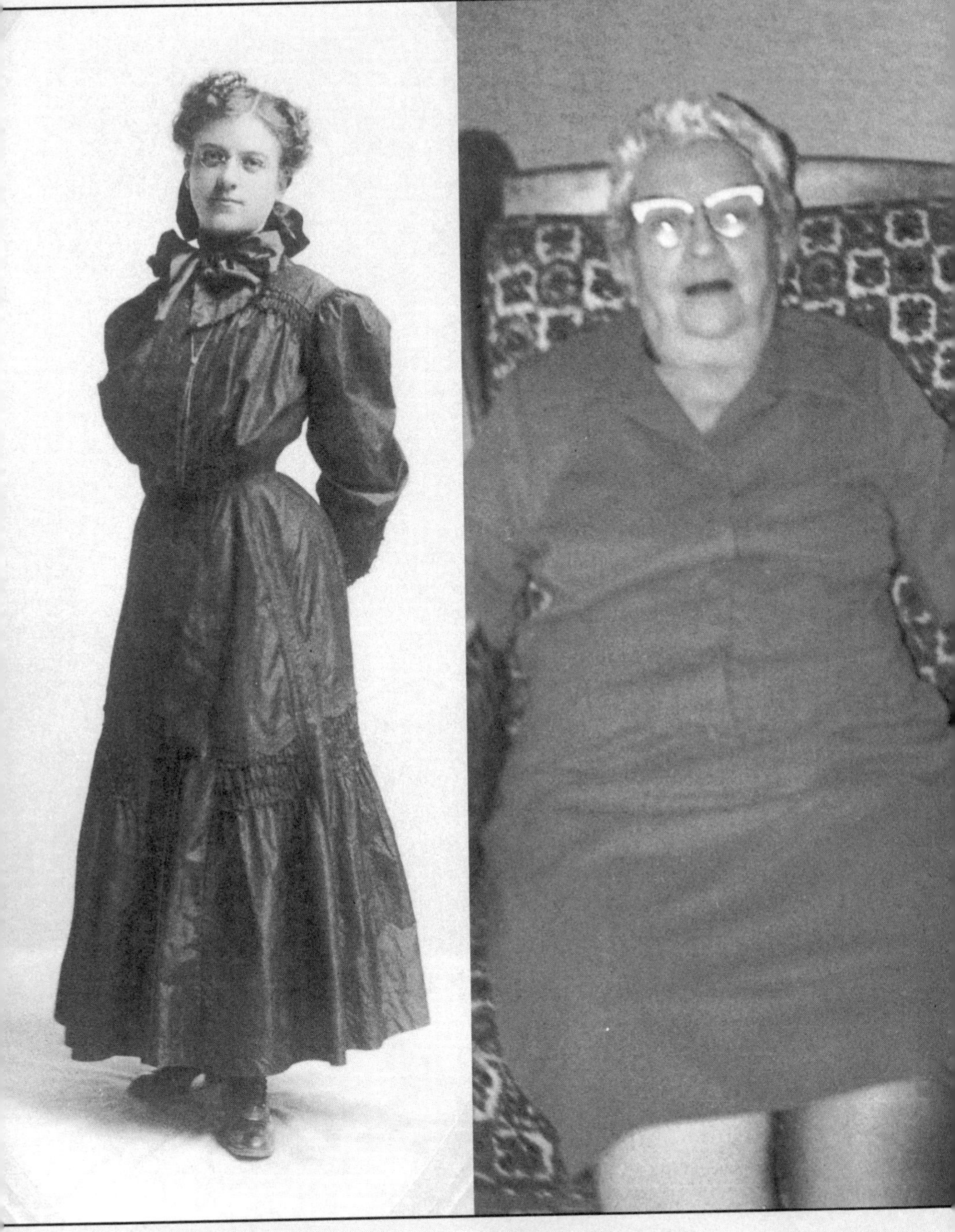

Left: Annabelle, before she went on the road.

Right: Annabelle, after she apparently ate her act.

8

LILLIPUT

APRIL 21ST, 2004

Hire film student, Blake Webster, to shoot 6-month documentary of me losing weight and learning how to create new, more beautiful life and be honest with self.

Spend $40,000 on film equipment to outfit selves like fully professional documentary film crew.

Buy cute stickers to put on camera cases, strike deal with Blake to shoot 7 days a week for 6 months.

View self as new rival to Michael Moore—only heavier subject matter.

APRIL 22ND, 2004

New tabloid shot of me on cover, claim now weigh 290 pounds.

First day of documentary shooting. Big basket delivered to house from well-known diet product company, beckoning me to come on board and be new poster girl. Product not acceptable for now-seasoned docu-

mentarian. Product in pill form, and no money could get documentarian interested in pill diet. Especially when documentarian's next film could be whistle-blowing of big pill company.

Proud of documentarian's personal integrity—used big basket as firewood holder.

APRIL 27TH, 2004

Offer comes in to play fat mother of Ricki Lake in TV sitcom and fat grandmother to two children. Have not played grandmother yet in career, and not played mother of 37-year-old child.

Like script—very funny. Know writers, very talented. Get word new sitcom filmed on same stage as Cheers *and* Frasier. *Good luck omen, sign from God. Decide fat grandma is in cards.*

MAY 6TH, 2004

Costume fitting for new fat grandmother show. Wardrobe mistress asked sizes, said 14s and 16s. Wardrobe mistress with apparent death wish gathered sizes 18 to 22.

When 18 to 22s were too big, wardrobe mistress feigned ignorance and denied using rags as "background" information, explaining she'd been told those were correct sizes. Wardrobe mistress will not have job on old Cheers *stage if new show goes to series.*

The hardest part of being fat is finding clothes in a normal store. In fact, once you creep over size 14, you're pretty much shit outta luck. And let's face it, in Hollywood or Beverly Hills, anything over an 8 is all but impossible to find. Asian women dump the most jack in Beverly Hills . . . well, Asian women do not come in sizes above a 4.

It seems that poorer women come in sizes above size 14, thus one can find lots of cheap clothes, but really not a lot of couture fat girl clothes. So a lot of my shopping has been reduced to Target, Walmart, and Lane Bryant. This is sort of the good and bad news of being portly. (Can women be portly?) Okay, being a lardass. Bad news, only giant sizes, good news, cheap clothes.

For the past 2 years I've thrived on cheap, fat girl clothes with elastic waists. At Target and Walmart clothes come in large, extra-large, XX-large, XXX-large, and perhaps quad-X. The fact is that any of these giant pants, above 1X, can be worn by someone weighing in at 200 or someone weighing in at 400. The waistbands could easily stretch from 38 inches to 54 inches or more.

In countries where the people are very poor and temperatures extremely cold, I've heard of families of five actually sleeping in one, size triple-X, pair of pants for warmth.

Another advantage to a triple-X is anonymity. At a moment's notice, if threatened with being spotted by an old high school friend with a still-hot body, or an extremely attractive man who shouldn't see you yet in a triple-X, you can whip the triple X over your head, drop down to your knees, and pose as a bag of dirty laundry waiting to be picked up by a service.

In my bleakest moments, I like to think of people with the opposite problem of the triple-X.

Like my beloved daughter, Lillie, when she came to us at 3 days old.

Lillie was so tiny that no real baby clothes would fit her. She was a wild-looking creature. Her head was odd-shaped, kind of wind-blown looking. Her eyes were huge and blue, lips full and pouty. Her tiny body was so tiny that the elastic waists of size minus triple X baby clothes would droop around her body like an empty sack of potatoes. I tried doll clothes, but the necks were too tight. (Who knew that dolls have out-of-proportion, skinny necks?) And most doll clothes are made of polyester and other man-made synthetic scratchy materials, not suited for my sweet baby.

For years I'd collected antique, vintage pillowcases, simple white cases with crocheting, embroidery, and appliqué on the bottoms. I'm sure my collection was in excess of 50 of these beauties. As I looked at the pillowcases while I made the bed next to Lillie, a very exciting idea swept over me. One that would rate right up there with the invention of Target triple-X's for big girls. If tents would work for giant girls, isn't it possible pillow cases would work for negative triple-X'ers?

I rode the ferry to the mainland, as we live on an island. I purchased 20 or 30 baby T-shirts, the tiniest size newborn T's available. Long sleeved, three-quarter sleeved, and a few short sleeved. I brought them home on the afternoon ferry and got busy. With a bassinet beside me, and Lillie in tow, my friend Sharon Ashley and I proceeded to crop the baby T's and cut the top seams out of the pillowcases. Now the pillowcases looked like tubes. We gathered all the tops and then pinned them to the bottoms of the cropped baby T's. Then we sewed them all up. Lillie had 24 baby dresses by the next evening—gorgeous, soft, hand-embroidered, crocheted, appliquéd dresses, more beautiful than some of the finest christening gowns I've seen in Italy or Paris. And more importantly, they fit!

To this day, Lillie is quite the fashion connoisseur. Exquisite, refined taste, individual, yet fashionable.

Ironically, however, Lillie is the biggest critic of my triple-X'er elastic Target pants. Hiding them, threatening to burn them, and laughing at them at every turn.

"Mama, no one should ever wear pants like these. They make you look way fatter than you are. Mama, just wear a skirt. Skirts make you look the smallest. And Mama, stop wearing giant shirts and sweaters, especially with your giant fat pants. You think they hide your butt, but they just make your butt look bigger."

You would think that a child whose mother had toiled over making her 24 teeny, tiny baby dresses, would show a little more respect for her fat-assed mama's special concerns.

Maybe it would better serve Mama if Lillie could take some antique sheets with embroidery or appliqué around the hems, seam them up on one side, making the sheets into large tubes. Then gathering the tops of the tubes and sewing them to the bottoms of some lovely boatnecked or V-necked T-shirts, size XL. That's right, why doesn't Lillie repay the favor by belting out 15 or 20 giant christening gowns for her dear old mom?

God, what's wrong with kids these days? No imagination? Or do they just not know how to sew?

Pippi Longstocking ain't got nothin' on me!

I'll take that blue-eyed doll—the one up there on that shelf next to that horrifying black-haired doll.

Mama, did you steal those fat pants from a clown?

9

Divine Attention

May 17th, 2004

Shot fat grandma sitcom "before live audience." Always made me laugh as opposed to shot sitcom "before dead audience." Felt renewed confidence in self and talent. Audience very alive, very receptive. Felt in glory. Felt assured show would be picked up for long-running new hit TV series.

Lost 5 pounds in 1 week and stopped smoking.

Thought of possibility of future sex with new rise to personal stardom. No time 'til men would beat stage door #25 down to get in sitcom grandma's pants.

I turned 10 and I was certain of two things—I was a flat-chested, big-butted buffoon, and no boy would ever be interested in something that was that off the mark.

I was a competitive swimmer on the Wichita swim club. I was not a great swimmer and not a lousy swimmer, just a swimmer. I don't know exactly how my family got roped into this monotonous sport, but I vaguely recall it had something to do with the summer I accidentally set fire to a field adjacent to the YMCA, where I was supposed to be frolicking in the pool.

Some boys I didn't know had firecrackers. They were paying a bit of attention to me, and I was soaking it up like the self-loathing sponge I'd become. These new playboys were sort of flirting with me, teasing me, snapping me with their damp towels, but all sort of vying for my attention somehow.

Showing off.

One was a cartwheeler, one said he was out of cigarettes but he could sure use one, and the one I fancied the most looked a little like Jesus, which I've since discovered all bad boys, homeless men, and leading actors look like. Blue eyes; slightly long, slightly greasy hair; aquiline noses. Businessmen, lawyers, doctors, Wall Street guys never ever look like Jesus. Just actors, the homeless, and random serial killers like Johnny Depp, James Dean, Kris Kristofferson, and Charles Manson.

The Jesus guys are somehow the guys we want to pursue, now aren't they? In our sick little minds we love them. Professional types always look a little like psychiatrists to me . . . like something is stuck permanently up their rectums, and their eyes are always a little dead, a little sharklike, like Hitler, Wundt, Mengele, Howard Stern, or Scott Peterson.

I was actually afraid of firecrackers, but knowing this could possibly be my last chance at Jesus love and the affections of some real men, I feigned "joy of firecrackers," downright exhilaration of firecrackers.

Look at me, look at me, Jesus and Mark and Luke and Judas, look at me, I'm the queen of firecrackers. The duchess of black cats. The mistress of M-80s. Oh yes, boys, I can run with the best of you, these little ole things don't scare me one bit, not one damn bit! Give me the punk, I'll light 'em up and spit 'em out. They'll fly outta my hands like a Howitzer repeating, repeating, repeating, repeating. Yee ha! Look at me, boys, look at me! I'm pretty and skinny when I throw firecrackers, aren't I? I'm a downright firecracker myself, aren't I?

"Glee" is the correct word for what I'd become around these "new" boys. I'm shocked that my eyes were not rolling around in my head like marbles going down a drainpipe. Perhaps they were, but I wouldn't have known. I was lost, gonzo, high on the attention of the scraggly haired, other-side-of-the-track boys.

Caught up in my reverie of self-absorbed psychosis, I neglected to see flames coming from my left peripheral zone. I'd neglected to yet realize this was for real, that I started a real fire. I laughed "ha ha!" in the face of fire.

I yelled, "Oh come on, a little grass fire never hurt anyone!"

Woo hoo! Yee ha! I'm a pyromaniac lunatic, but, by God, Jesus loves me, he can't get enough of me! Kirstie Lou is the center of his universe!

Through my gritted maniacal teeth and possessed engorged eyes I could see the boys had diverted their swell attention elsewhere. They had taken off their towels and were beating out a now-immense field fire.

My zealotlike grimace melted into terror as I realized the flames were out of control and headed for the neighborhood YMCA.

Is this how I would go down in history? The stupid big-butted girl who only had the brief attention of a few trailer park apostles? The breast-less girl who burned down the Young Men's Christian Association, depriving young Christian men from miles around the luxury of a 50-meter pool with the fellowship of a thousand-odd other young Christian men? Not to mention the Christian women?

And would the headline of the *Wichita Eagle and Beacon* read: "Really Flat 10-Year-Old Who Could Turn Out Fat If She Doesn't Watch It, with Big Bottom and No Real Boyfriend, Torches Young Men's Christian Association, Causing Kansans Everywhere to Hit Deep Depression, Rendering Most of Midwest Population Hopelessly Suicidal"?

I began crying, wailing really. Like those very bratty, desperate children who don't get what they want at Macy's. Ugly-face crying—lips distorted like a wax candle melting in the sun. Eyes frozen shut, snot running down my face, dripping into the candle-waxed scream. If I'd had hair of any length, I would have pulled it out by the roots, like I'd seen a woman do when I was 7, after she'd run over a neighborhood kid and killed him.

Divine torture of the soul had engulfed me, until I heard Jesus speak.

"Hey crybaby. Hey, stop bawlin', will ya? It's out."

It's out? Blubber, blubber. It's out?

I peered out from underneath my tear-soaked eyelashes, and all the "new" boys were looking at me. Was it too late for me to cover? Had they seen and heard all the histrionics? It was pretty obvious they had when they all cracked up laughing at me, pointing and shouting, "Hey bawl baby, you almost burned down the YMCA!"

"Hey dumbass, stop your snifflin', you dumbass pyro."

The last words Jesus spoke to me were those, "You dumbass pyro . . ."

I was very glad that the fire was out. I could hardly hate the motley trailer park disciples, even if they were making fun of me, for in truth, they saved all those Christians and their swimming pool, and me from prison and ridicule.

Sometimes I wonder if those boys know that the girl who almost torched the YMCA back then is me. Sometimes I wonder if they ever read *Star* magazine and say, "Hey Jesus, ain't that fatty on the cover the same girl who almost burned down the YMCA with a firecracker 40 years ago?"

"Yeah, her ass looks the same, Luke, I think she is the same gal."

"What a dumbass."

You said it, Jesus, what a dumbass.

Top: My favorite attention was from my dad, even on a bad hair day.

Bottom: Lillian looks disturbed. Maybe she's wondering if I got switched at birth.

I don't know why I love attention so much—
my folks weren't in show biz or anything.

10

Mamsley

May 24th, 2004

Big offer to do Oprah Winfrey Book Club movie for CBS. Okay to be fat. Character is over hill, overweight veterinarian who has lost vivacity for life. Eagerly begin negotiations.

Decide to send video to Oprah Winfrey for Nate to do kitchen makeover. Have Blake turn documentary camera on me, and create plea for new Nate kitchen.

Have lost no weight on documentary diet. Have much footage of me eating and playing with children and animals. Start smoking again to look more like gritty docu-maker, caliber of Sundance film festival and Palme d'Or in Cannes.

June 8th, 2004

Filming going well in Winnipeg. Playing fat over-hill veterinarian, good call.

Went to benefit for police officer killed on duty. Star *magazine re-*

porter there asking people at benefit what they thought about me being so fat. Star *reporter forgets to interview family and friends of fallen officer.*

Sent memo to God.

"Don't let Star *reporter into Heaven to mingle with other clientele. Please send downstairs for photo op of Lucifer. Remind reporter to get huge shot of Satan's ass and shot of own head up self's ass. Photo op shot worth $500,000 U.S."*

June 10th, 2004

On cover of Star *magazine. Photographers hid in woods on set. New weight 302 pounds.*

Called God, asked if had received last memo.

Said, "Don't worry, doors to heaven always open to fatties, but Star *guys? . . . Hah, hah, hah, hah, hah!"*

God, I love the way God laughs.

My son, True, has taken to calling me "Mamsley." Who knows why or where he got the tag. But now 90 percent of the time I am addressed as "Mamsley."

Someone at True's school told him last year that he was fat. For a short while he developed quite an obsession with this lie.

First of all, he's not fat. Not even close to fat.

When "Mamsley" asked who at school had said that he was fat, he protected his invalidator adamantly, refusing to reveal his or her identity. I suspect there wasn't really a school source. This took place around the time all the rags began running fat photos of me. And I worried that he worried that if he were photographed with me by the paparazzi, he might publicly be called fat, too. This thought broke my heart.

He told "Mamsley" that he had to immediately begin an intensive exercise program and cut out all carbs and fats from his diet. When I told him that he was a "growing boy" and that it was perfectly natural to beef up a bit and then grow into it, then beef up and then grow, etc., he alluded to the fact that I was a liar by saying, "Mamsley, you are a liar."

He began to lift things—weights, dogs, cats, and furniture. He would not put anything in his mouth containing carbs, fat, or sugar, except for Quizno's sandwiches, which he had deduced are close enough to Subway's, and that Jared, the spokesperson for Subway, had lost weight on those.

More than several times he pounded his head and lamented, "I'm fat, I'm ugly, I'm stupid." Something I'd thought thousands of times in the last 3 years about myself. Something I'd begun thinking when I was just a year older than my son.

When I was 13, I saw a placard in a store window back in Kansas. It said that a "professional model photographer" would be in town the following Saturday to take photos of girls who would like to be models. Very apropos since the clothing store was called "The Model." There was also a contest—the most model-like girl chosen would go to New York City for a full, real photo shoot.

I had had men around the age of 40 tell me my entire 13-year life that I had beautiful bedroom eyes. And some even said I was pretty. Although I now suspect each of these men to have been pedophiles, I soaked up the admiration at the time.

I knew my body was not fawnlike. Not like Twiggy or Cheryl Tiegs or Jean Shrimpton. I knew it wasn't breathtaking like my favorite Russian model, Verushka. However, this placard that read at its end, "You could be the world's next most famous model" made me wonder.

What if I looked like an idiot in person—but what if this profound "model" photographer could make me look like Verushka in a stunning "model" photograph? What if I was the world's next most famous "model" and I didn't even realize it?

The following Saturday morning I filed in with a few other unlikely suspects. Apparently, there were several hundred unknown "models" in Wichita. Apparently, Wichita, Kansas, was about to be discovered as the dumping ground, the treasure trove, the "model" mecca of the entire known world.

I knew some of the girls there. One who always asked me where I got my clothes. When I told her my mother had made this or that outfit, or I had gotten them at K-Mart, she would smirk and say, "Oh, cute city."

Cute city. What the hell does that mean?

I still don't have a clue.

Another girl was one of those "it" girls. The breathtakingly beautiful Bad Girl of East High School. It was rumored that she'd been having sex since age 12, and that she was also very good at "doing it."

Other than a few odd skanks, I was clearly the dumbest-looking future "model" in the store. But I kept reminding myself—I'm not fat, I'm flat like Twiggy, I'm the only one here with short hair (like that was an asset), and I, I have one other thing the other girls don't. I have bedroom eyes.

The photographer's assistant chose a sort of Edwardian-slash-military look for me. Sort of mod, sort of British street girl. I clearly remember putting my hand on my right hip and contorting my body like I'd seen Verushka do in the *Vogue* magazine my next-door neighbor had shown me.

It felt right, you know?

I glared that special model glare at the photographer. My body was twisted and professional. I beamed him with my smoky bedroom eyes.

Flash! One shot.

Hell. One shot was all I would need to bring those New York photo editors to their knees.

All week long I looked through fashion magazines borrowed from my next-door neighbor's slutty sister visiting from Dallas, Texas. I counted the seconds until the following Saturday, when I would see my photo posted in the "models" window and hear the word that I was rushing off to New York, hair a blowin', for my full-length photo shoot. And from there on to, who knows . . . Paris, Milan, or even to Russia to runway alongside Verushka.

I woke up early on Saturday and didn't eat much. Couldn't. My new agency wouldn't want me to.

I walked a mile to "The Model." It wasn't snowing or sleeting, and I didn't have to endure the harsh elements like Abe Lincoln, but it was a long walk filled with anticipation.

The last hundred yards felt like I was walking through Jell-O. Slow motion. I reminded myself that I had BEDROOM EYES. I HAD BEDROOM EYES. A newfound confidence poured over me. Something like I'd never experienced before. Very zen. Very Buddha.

Be the model, be the model, be the model.

I AM THE MODEL!

With the certainty of Guatamma Siddhartha Buddha, I leapt in front of The Model's display window. My eyes danced from photo to photo; my matrixlike conviction began to dissolve into my usual state of introversion and embarrassment as I realized my photo wasn't on the placard.

But then in a surge of Bodhi-like strength, I cleverly thought, *The winner, the winner's not on the placard, now is it? Just randoms displayed with a tongue-in-cheek "good effort girls!" But the winner, well, I'm sure they're waiting to reveal the winner in a big ceremony. That's right, I'll be accepting my New York modeling contract at a big ceremony.*

Girls were buzzing around looking at their photos. I saw some of them. They actually were pretty amazing, pretty "professional," and many were pretty gorgeous.

I asked the assistant for my photo. She smiled a huge smile.

"Oh my God, I can't wait to show you. You're the girl with those beautiful bedroom eyes!"

She laid the key to the next 20 years of my life as a world-renowned model in my hands.

My heart skipped a beat.

This is it.

This is the glory I've waited so long for. Here's my ticket out of Wichita, Kansas, and right smack-dab on the cover of Vogue *magazine.*

Cherish this moment Kirstie—revel in it.

I looked at the snapshot . . .

I can honestly say that if I had a 45 in my pocket, I would have used it at that moment, blasting my bedroom eyes across "The Model," out its back door, and into the next county.

Here was this picture of this dykey-looking short-haired girl. This girl who not only didn't look like a world-renowned model, but a girl who didn't even look like a girl.

The haircut that I had been assured by my beauty operator aunt looked like Mary Quant, actually looked like a Nazi helmet with fur on it.

My contorted body looked exactly like that—contorted. I had no idea I was that limber. I didn't know anyone was, except circus personnel.

The sexy glare I gave the photographer looked more like a demonically possessed hypnotizer of small children and cats.

The "mod" outfit made me look like Humpty Dumpty on acid.

And the bedroom eyes? They were clenched so tightly in my supermodel, sex-bomb grimace that no one could have possibly known if they were blue or green or brown or even black, for that matter.

The Beautiful Bad Girl won the contest, even though her breasts were way too big to be a model, in my opinion.

She went to New York. She also later stole the love of my 15-year-old life, for sport. She also moved to Los Angeles and dated the lead singer in one of the biggest bands in the world, and he wrote a song about her and used her name in it.

My son has stopped worrying about his weight. He grew 3 inches in the last 6 months and hasn't mentioned his body again.

The other week he was looking at a horrible picture of me on the cover of *Star* and said, "They are wrong, Mamsley. I think you're beautiful. I think you look like a model."

Who knew that the cover of a rag mag would end up meaning more to me than the cover of *Vogue*?

Mamsley, did you go down the drain?

Top: Give me the guitar, Mamsley. You look like an idiot!

Bottom: Mamsley, why, why, why do you make us dress like Russian immigrants for photo shoots?

11

Farewell to Lillian

June 12th, 2004

Blake says someone on phone wants to speak to me. Answered while Blake filmed. Oprah is going to do kitchen! Nate coming to Los Angeles on August 1st.

Was exhilarated!

Ecstatic—dreams coming true. What decided, coming true. What planned, happening.

Was one with physical and spiritual universe. Except for million-odd Winnipeg mosquitoes, terrible pain of missing children, and hearing news not picking up stage 25 fat grandma series, all is right in world.

June 20th, 2004

Children arrive today. Excited about Winnipeg zoo. Excited about trip to Maine in 10 days at end of filming. Excited about future Oprah kitchen. New rag out today. Children upset and consoling, trying to tell me, "It's okay, Mama, you don't look that fat."

New rag weight, 320 pounds. New rag disease, confirmed by fictitious doctor, morbid obesity. Now realize is confirmed, am going to die from fake rag weight, fake rag disease. Dive into despair.

Ten minutes later despair turned to glory. Big hotshot Showtime head bought Fat Actress. *Wants to begin filming in September.*

Celebrate with children and nanny at fancy Croatian restaurant. Celebrate with risotto, fettuccine, fried calamari, steak Florentine, and tiramisu. Wish had popcorn balls for dessert also.

Finally have come out of cocoon. Finally am full-fledged fat actress with own new show. Bring on crippling, humiliating photos and diseases. Bring on degraded rag reporters and photographers who will spend eternal lives in hell—"Fat Actress" in heaven.

The Beverly Hills diet—that's the diet I'd just completed in October of 1981. By god, I was hell-bent on being a movie star, and I'd whittled myself down to fighting weight—a tiny 117 pounds, and a size four pants—a real size four, by today's measures, probably a size two.

The Beverly Hills diet consisted of a different fruit all day, each day. One day pineapple, one day papaya, one day pineapple and papaya, yadda, yadda, yadda. My body dropped weight like nobody's business on this diet—my skin looked like a baby's ass, and I had endless energy.

I'd been in for three auditions in the big times—Paramount's *Star Trek II: The Wrath of Khan*. I'd never worked one day as an actress. My days were spread between three jobs—interior decorating, selling hats for Caspell Twid, and being a housekeeper for several people I'd met along the way.

But this was the Big League and I knew it.

I'd given myself 1 year to become a working actor, and by that I meant an actor who got a job, became famous, and did only acting for a living.

Shortly before Halloween, this very handsome fellow asked me out on a date. I pretty much knew I had no interest in him. But again, I was looking for fun, not marriage or love. Just fun.

Of course, sex without love never was fun to me, but I really wanted it to be. I wanted to get better at meaningless encounters. I wanted to be like the other new California girls I'd met—free, slutty, and cavalier. So I accepted this date with Mr. Wrong, with high expectations of nothing happening.

Around 6:00 P.M., I started feeling very weird. Insane actually—actually insane. Like a caged bird slamming around the universe, I could literally be nowhere comfortably.

I wandered from room to room, wired, agitated. Maybe I'd been poisoned, or maybe the 300 pineapples and papayas I'd eaten in the last 3 weeks had eaten into my brain. The diet made promises that enzymes would eat all the fat out of my body.

What if they'd eaten the fat out of my brain, too? The necessary brain fat to cushion my left and right lobes from ricocheting off of my skull?

Pacing and pacing. Standing up, lying down, fidgeting endlessly. My universe was coming unglued. As I lay in my titty-pink bedroom, with white ruffled sheets for curtains, I was quietly going mad.

I hollered out to my roommate Alice in the next room.

"Hey Alice, can you call this number and tell this guy I'm sick? I can't go out tonight after all."

I can't go out tonight and spend meaningless time pretending I'm interested in your life or your history. I can't go out tonight and flirt endlessly with you, knowing that neither of us has anything of value to offer each other. Instead I must stay home inside my pink womb and slowly, helplessly sink into the bliss of certifiable insanity.

"Can you make that call, Alice?"

Alice made the call. He said he hoped I felt better soon, and maybe we could go out the next night.

Yeah, right.

If they don't come and take me away in a straight jacket between now and then. Yes, I'd love to do a meaningless dinner tomorrow.

My roommate Alice interrupted the romp with my demons about 20 minutes after canceling my meaningless date. She announced that my sister was on the phone, and that she was pretty upset.

My sister succinctly and with great precision told me that my parents had been in a car wreck.

"Mom is dead and Dad is dying," were her exact words.

"You need to come home."

Instantly and oddly enough, my universe went dead quiet. Like the air before a tornado—just dead quiet.

My insanity was not insanity at all, but the truth of what was really happening to my family, to my father, to my mother. The chaos of a universe turned inside out.

The funny thing about human beings is that they possess an

age-old defense mechanism—shock. How calm I was when I drove across town to borrow $500 to get a midnight flight to Wichita. How kind Sue and Mike were to loan me the late-night cash, and how lucky I was that people still had cash and not just credit cards.

I can't remember who drove me to the airport that night. I don't remember making the reservations. I do know I flew all night and had varied stops around the country, and that I finally ended up in Kansas at about 6:00 A.M.

Another funny thing about humans is that in times of great loss and emotion, something in them kicks into survival mode. Sleep and food do not exist, and neither does time.

When I arrived at the hospital, my cousins and aunts and uncles were lined up in a row in the waiting room. My sister and brother were at one end together. The next thing I remember is looking at the floor with my head in my hands, waiting, just waiting to see if my dad was going to live or die.

Nothing was said for the longest time. Then a thought occurred to me.

"Where were they going?"

"To a Halloween party," my sister answered.

Another long silence ensued.

Then the curiosity consumed me.

"What were they dressed as?"

Again, without making contact, except with the floor, my sister spoke. "They went as the Odd Couple. Dad was the Grand Wizard of the KKK, and Mom went as a pickaninny."

The domino effect ensued, laughter spreading like the wave at a Chief's game.

We all laughed for a good long time, and then we cried, and then we laughed again.

One thing my mom was not short on was humor and wit. And now, in her final act of stand-up, she had been taken to heaven dressed like a little black girl with pigtails and all.

It's pretty hard to stay consumed with grief when that is the last image of your mother. I actually think it's what made the blow of her being killed by a drunk driver a little softer.

I wish sometimes that the woman who killed my mother that night could have known her. And sometimes wish she had known about my mother's costume because maybe she, too, would know that my mother was a pretty funny person.

I'd like this lady to know that the mother she killed would have been the first person to scream at her for driving drunk and killing her, but also would have been the first person to have forgiven her.

I hope somehow the woman knows that.

When I returned to Los Angeles 3 days later, after my mother's funeral and after waiting for my dad to come out of intensive care, I weighed 113 pounds. I auditioned one last time for *Star Trek II*. The director, Nicholas Meyer, told me on the spot that I had the role. I always thought that was very kind of him.

After this whole ordeal I realized I'd learned a very good lesson about life . . . the Beverly Hills diet was really effective, but there's nothing like death to take off those last 4 stubborn pounds.

Top: Lillian scores one for short girls who like to stand in puddles.

Bottom Left: Nurse Lillian to the rescue!

Bottom Right: You are deeply missed . . . however if you are wearing that hat in heaven, please don't refer to us by first and last name.

12

SKY CLASS

JUNE 26TH, 2004

Movie almost over. Children antsy for Maine. Fat Actress antsy to get on plane. Old fear kicked in full force. Not fear of flying. Fear of 41,000-foot accidental plunge to ground. Begin desperate attempts to rearrange booked flights. Sweating profusely. Not sleeping well.

Now worried about fuck-up of reservations, children's seats not beside mine. Want to murder inept travel agent. Lose 4 pounds in next 5 days.

What is up with airline seats these days? And also, are my arms getting shorter? The last 40 flights I've taken have been in infant car seats. The arms of the seats are so close in that I can barely wedge into my seat. When I flew to Maine last summer in coach, I literally had to put the arm up on the seat next to me and leave it that way for the entire flight. If I'd put it down, I would have taken a slice right off the edge of my thigh.

And first class is just as bad. Why, I used to be able to sit one of my babies next to me in a first-class seat. No longer! No, these cheap sons of bitches at the airlines are fucking us royally, people. I think they think we are stupid and that we haven't noticed how they have slowly but surely whittled and chiseled seats ever so covertly, inch by inch, aisle by aisle, until we are all packed up like sailors in a strip club.

And those tiny airplane bathrooms are so miniature that the dream of being in the mile high club is now reserved only for those who have no arms and legs.

In the last 2 years, each time I've tried to reach my arm around my ass, to, well, wipe my bottom, I've been so cramped I could barely reach the location to be cleansed! Now, my arms have sure as hell not gotten shorter, so it has to be their damn, cramped lavatories.

I'm really exhausted by the whole issue. But as I do have to fly frequently for work, I feel a letter is in order:

Dear Mr. Airline,

On behalf of all Americans, I would just like to say "the jig is up!" We've listened to your poor, poor me, terrorist this and security that bullshit now for 3 years, since 9/11.

Wah, wah, wah.

How you've lost this money because of this, because of that . . . the price of gas, the cost of half-full planes. Well, Mr. Airline, let me just say this to you—we paid billions of dollars for your half-assed airlines long before 9/11.

Your shitty food, your smart-ass personnel, your lost luggage, tardy flights, lengthy layovers, and stinky restrooms. So don't give us this new line of shit about how fucking hard up you assholes are! We've been at your relentlessly greedy mercy since planes took to the skies and now, now this?

These little fucking go-cart seats from a children's amusement park?

You think we really are so stupid that we haven't noticed the baby high chairs you pass off as first-class seats?

We won't take it anymore!

We want full-fledged wide-load bucket seats, Lazyboy recliner style. We want to be able to sit our asses down in big, wide-bodied seats when we fly coast to coast. And our brothers back in coach? Hell, they're immobilized back there in what you mother fuckers so generously refer to as coach.

We don't know what kind of coaches you've been riding around in lately, but what you call "coach" should more accurately be called cubbyhole. That's right, "cubbyhole" class, because that is the real size of your second-rate seats.

And economy class? Sweet Jesus. Those seats should just be called "jump seats." Like tiny Murphy beds that actually pull down from the oxygen mask area above the "cubbyhole" class passengers. The "jump seat" passengers could lay in the fetal position in these jump seats, tucking their legs in tightly so as not to dangle them down into the faces of the cubbyhole classers below them.

And perhaps you could then sell the floor space to "floor space" class passengers. These would make excellent children's areas, especially if you required *all* carry-on bags to be stowed in the storage bins overhead. Then young children could be placed under all of the seats and used as footrests by the "first-class passengers," hereafter to be referred to as the "dumb fuckers" in the little seats up front who paid three grand for their tickets to New York.

Boarding one of your airline's flights would sound something like this:

"Ladies and gentlemen, flight number 2 is now boarding at gate 18. Will all children and people who are catatonic or those who are paralyzed report for pre-boarding on 'floor class'?

"We'll then ask for all jump seat passengers to board, and we'll request that you remove your shoes as not to kick people below you in the heads.

"We will then board all of our 'cubbyholers.' And don't forget to add up those frequent cubbyholer miles.

"And lastly, but certainly not leastly, we'll board all you 'dumb fuckers' who paid three times more than everyone else paid just because you thought you were going to get a bigger chair and more food.

"Oh, and yes, we almost forgot about you 'stand-by' flyers. You don't have a fucking prayer to get to your destination, unless we lose some of this baggage that we love to leave behind, in which case we can probably shove you into some niche between the dog and cat kennels. Thank you for flying the friendly skies . . ."

Sincerely,
Your platinum elite member, "Dumb Fucker" class,
Kirstie Louise Alley

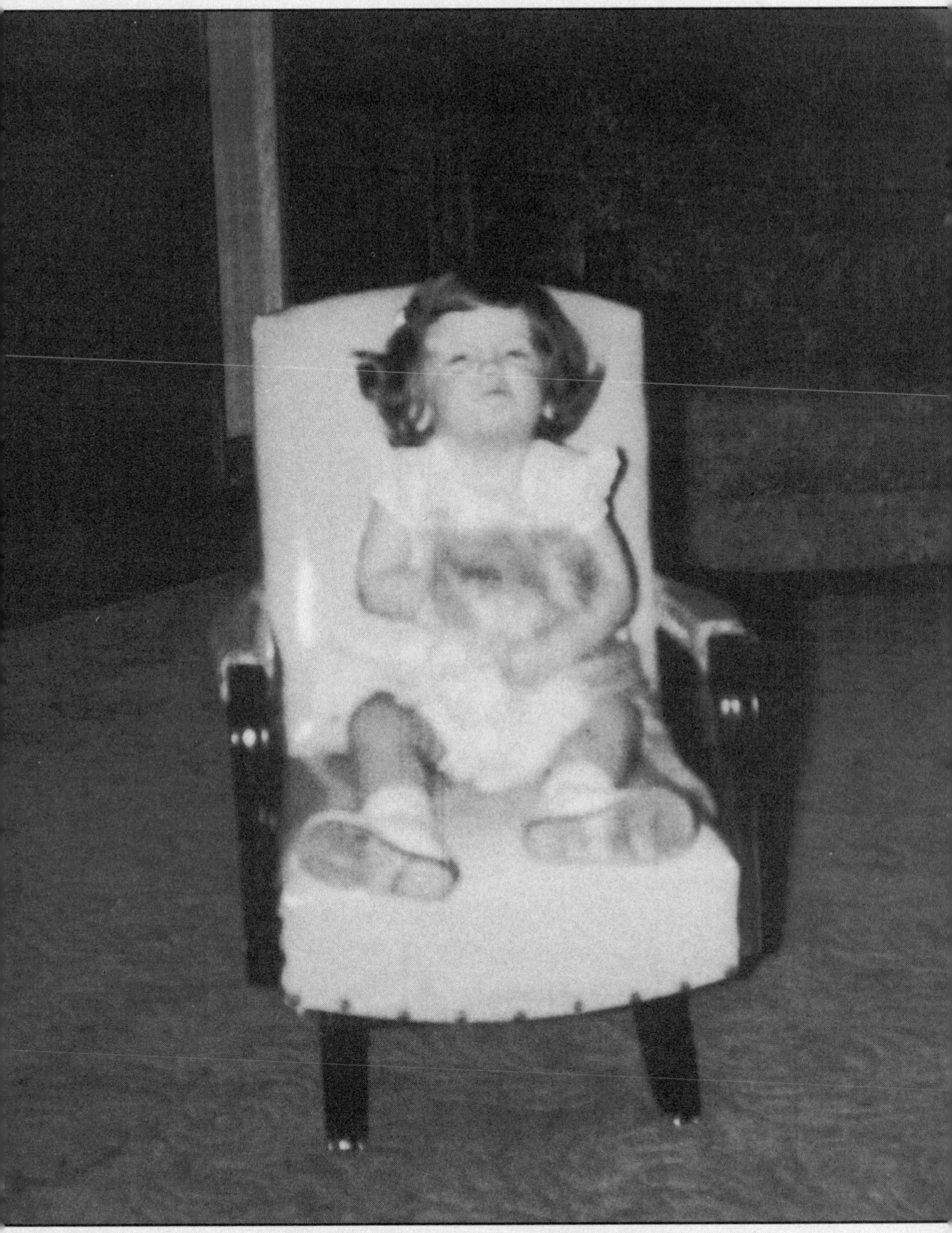

Satisfied first-class customer in wide-bodied seat.

13

GO HEMP YOURSELF!

JULY 1ST, 2004

Spring for private plane to fly self and children to Maine for month of July. Great day to fly. Beautiful weather. Minimal fear . . . was not overridden by gremlin sitting on plane's wing.

Private plane was beautiful, perfect, especially for big actress with new, potential hit series!

Plane and all passengers aboard arrive safely in Maine. Ah Maine, glorious Maine. A smell like no other, fresh and balsamy. Newly mown grass, lilacs, peonies, and salt air.

True and Lillie told scary stories. Ended with being terrified and having to leave lights on to sleep.

Good, deep, children-in-tow, out-of-plane, Maine sleep.

JULY 5TH, 2004

Tutoring for True. Cooking lessons for Lillie. Jumping on water trampoline off of dock in ocean for all. Docu-filming for Blake, post-holiday eating for me.

Visit to cemetery to scare selves even more. Slept with all lights in house on. Think of adding new man to family to prevent night terror for self and children.

JULY 8TH, 2004

Guests Lisa, Scott, Robin, Art, four children, and Dad arrive. Also three extra Welsh corgis.

Decided good idea to have corgi reunion. My dog Maybelle, her husband Marty, the two corgi puppies I'd kept, Posy and Lizzie. Then Robin's corgi, Lizzy, who is sister of Maybelle, and two other of Maybelle's puppies, Arrow and Beauty, now living with Lisa and Scott, and one other of Maybelle's puppies, Rufus, now living with friend Sharon Hall.

Eight corgis. Heavenly.

Will be first of yearly corgi reunions. How cozy.

JULY 9TH, 2004

Maybelle viciously attacked corgi #4, Robin's Lizzy, ripping sides, ears, and head. May's puppies joined in horrifying bloodbath. Corgis must now be separated for rest of corgi reunion.

Lizzy fine, in a lot of pain, but fine. Hate my dog Maybelle. If weren't mother of all other puppies would seriously think of inflicting same damage on her.

Friend Robin hating me and Maybelle. Tension so thick could be cut with glass pie cutter.

JULY 10TH, 2004

Get new offer to be national diet spokesperson. Contemplating offer while tasting food.

Maybelle and evil pack of offspring attack one of Lisa's corgis. Have corgis separated out and placed in five different locations.

Children had lemonade stand. Decorated it. Made $85.00. Cost of lemonade and fancy French cookies, $92.00.

Maybelle, Lizzie, Lizzy, Posy, and Beauty all in heat . . . bleeding over antique needlepoint rugs.

Ate 28 popsicles today.

JULY 15TH, 2004

Call from Showtime—need to come to island immediately and shoot in-house promo for release of Fat Actress.

Put Pampers with holes cut for tails on girl dogs as have bled on all chairs, sofas, and rugs in house.

Declined to do national diet program. Deem food too close to astronaut food without the fine taste of Tang.

JULY 21ST, 2004

Made giant slip and slide for children. Forty-feet wide by one-hundred-feet long. Giant sheet of thick plastic. Went well. Few children hit rocks. Had bleeding knees but not to be out-bled by Maybelle and three daughters.

Male corgis—Marty, Arrow, and Rufus—have been mounting Maybelle and girl pups 24-7. Makes one of human children, Mallory, sick to stomach. Is sitting by herself in car weeping. Hope

Mallory has different attitude when self gets mounted for first time.

Decide to stop eating sugar. Go on health food craze. Blood and humping ruining appetite anyway.

Selective eating, that's what I prefer to call diets. Selective eating has been an integral part of my life since I turned 15.

The types of selective eating I have engaged in could be organized, chronicled, and viewed like the Macy's Thanksgiving Day parade from the seventh floor of the Pierre Hotel, if the parade traveled past the Pierre.

I only mention the New York City–based Pierre Hotel because it is the only hotel I've ever stayed in, in New York—intentionally. I love this hotel like I love the memory of a dear friend, and vow never to betray my beloved hotel.

No, no, no, there is no other place for me. This place where I know all the staff and have, over the past 24 years, watched their children grow up, witnessed their families marry, and shared in their losses. This is my home in New York . . . even though my home prices out at $1,800 a night, corporate rate. My two bedroom, suite #627, is my home suite home while in the Big Apple.

Long ago I should have purchased an apartment there. I had a swell opportunity to do just that in 1999. My significant other at the time thought the Pierre too hoity-toity.

Anyway, if I could see the Macy's Thanksgiving Day parade from the Pierre Hotel's seventh-floor window, it would be of comparable length to the trail of "selective eating" programs I've partaken in these past 35-odd years.

Since I'm lingering like a mental cripple here momentarily at the Pierre hotel, let's begin here.

The tearoom at the Pierre is paradise. Many a violation of any of the various select programs I've been on has transpired in that big, gorgeous, hand-muraled, gilt-chaired, 40-foot ceilinged Duchess of a high tearoom. High teas of jasmine lipstick-tasting tea, finger sandwiches—the cucumber and the egg salad on pastry puffs being my two favorites—heavy clotted cream, scones with tiny currants, and a veritable treasure trove of miniature sugar plums.

At least 20 times in my life I recall creeping past the tearoom or running past it at the speed of light, so that I did not enter the grand ballroom of temptation.

Here are some of the "selective eating" programs I've gone astray on while staying at the Pierre:

1. The Scarsdale Diet
2. The Zone
3. The Master Cleanse
4. The Water Fast
5. The Egg and Grapefruit Diet
6. Fit for Life
7. The Sugarless Caramel Marshmallow Crèmes Diet
8. The Spirulina Diet
9. Optifast
10. Fruit juice fast
11. Vegetable juice fast
12. And my old standby, The Atkins Diet

The Atkins Diet has always been my fallback diet, for when all else fails. Only because I basically am starving to death and want an excuse for a good steak and some fine fried pork rinds. After I've Atkinized for 2 or 3 weeks and gotten good and full, I resort to the next fad selective eating program to come down the pike.

My favorite programs have included the "Master Cleanse." This consists of fasting on gallons of water with lemon, maple syrup, and cayenne pepper. It is pretty yummy, like a spicy lemonade.

But also included in this program is a daily dose of sea salt water, gulped down to "push" the poop and toxins from your body. This concoction of warm water and sea salt sounds harmless enough. But the weirdest thing happens when these two things mix together. It feels, not tastes, but feels, heavy and thick . . . like drinking warm blood might feel. My Master Cleanse fasts usually lasted from 20 to 50 days, but the blood was only consumed for the first 3 of the 20 to 50 days. It gave me reassurance that I would certainly never take up the hobby of vampirism.

My other all-time favorite was the Beverly Hills diet. First day, pineapple; second day, papaya; third day, pineapple and papaya. The real clincher of this diet was the future hope that one could consume massive amounts of chocolate cake, and then counter the effects with massive amounts of pineapple or papaya enzyme. Can't remember which it is that counters cake. Pasta and butter are devoured by pineapple enzymes—bromelain. Steaks are devoured by papaya enzyme.

This was a great program for dropping 14 pounds in 11 hours or less—spending 10 of those 11 hours on the toilet.

I invented a selective eating program myself once, and I loved it.

I combined the Atkins low- or no-carb diet with Fit for Life—a mostly high-carb vegetarian eating plan. This was the most delicious program of all of them.

I gained 11 pounds in 7 days on my self-invented program.

My least favorite eating program was the raw food program. This program is 10% diet and 90% religion, as these devotees really do believe you are what you eat. After 2 weeks of fermented raw meat, fermented (rotted, actually, in a bell jar) raw almonds, raw eggs mixed in raw cream, Stepford spaghetti made from raw carrots shredded into long strands, and raw butter slathered on raw buffalo meat, two things occurred. My energy and health felt like a million bucks. But my mental state felt like I should be living in a yurt on some acreage in Oregon with my husband Seth and my two kids Tree and Leaf.

All of my dreams of things like the Pierre tea, Christmas with real people with indoor lavatories, French restaurants, dates with Italians, softball games in Kansas, gone, gone, poof before my eyes.

There I would be at a summer softball game with a local Kansas boy running the bases. Then we would celebrate afterward. But not at the "Dairy Queen," and not at the "House of Pancakes or Pies." No, we would celebrate at the "House of Fermented Meat" or the "House of Pine Nuts" or, better yet, the "Airy-Fairy, Raw Dairy Queen."

It seems one certainly could extend his or her lifespan with this eating style, but who would want to extend it with you?

Raw food eaters need to band together and feed together. And ditto for cooked food folks. The two philosophies reach far beyond the kitchen.

Most raw food folk are also hemp advocates. They say hemp for shoes and clothes and blankets and such. But it's always a little odd that they also happen to be the biggest pot-smoking, Mary Jane–toking loadies on the West Coast.

"We worship hemp, we want hemp! Hemp will save the fucking world," they cry.

"Everything will be okay if everything is just made out of hemp! We fucking love hemp!"

They are basically the same group of people incarnate who also spent most of their lives in the 15th century in opium dens, later to reincarnate into the 1960s where they really, really, really believed if everyone just practiced free love and fucked everyone who walked past them the world would be okay.

"We love fucking everyone! We worship fucking. We fucking love fucking!"

These groups are not really new at all. They pop up once or twice in every century. These people are called INSANE.

But, if enough insane people band together, you have what are called townships, then towns, then cities, then countries, get it?

Not to say everyone everywhere in the world who eats only raw food is insane, or a free love fucker. However, if the hemp fits, wear it.

The Cocaine Diet

Top: The Swimmer's Diet

Bottom: The We-Didn't-Make-It-Into-Playboy Diet

The Let-Them-Eat-Cake Diet

14

Driving Miss Kirstie

JULY 23RD, 2004

Guests leave to return to Wichita and Connecticut. Heating, humping dogs and random children leave, too. Dad goes with brood. In come new guests, Michael, Denise, and daughter Paris. In come photo shoot crew—photographer and two publicists, one writer, five-odd stylists, hairdressers, and makeup artists for cover of People *magazine.*

Served them all variety of six cakes, three pies, lemonade, and sugar cookies. Lunch was sandwiches, chips, and sodas.

Looked radiant for fat girl. Ate remaining cakes, pies, cookies, and sandwiches while watched All about Eve.

Caught glimpse of self in mirror by TV. Pretty . . . still . . . well . . . pretty. Maybe sex this year. Yes, make note. Get mounted in '04.

Here was this thing I'd waited for my whole life. Here was the thing I'd reduced down to 115 pounds for. The thing my friend-slash-high-school-slut, who later became a senator's wife, had keenly taught me how to prepare for. The thing my mother had warned me of every day of my existence.

"IT."

I was prepared and ready for "it."

I was ready to do "it."

Fornication, fucking, humping, boning, boffing, or making love. That one—making love—makes me laugh the most.

I was ready for the rite of passage into my lily pink, pristine, virginal 17-year-old pussy.

I was ready to accept a penis, tool, bone, shaft, prick, dick, peter—a hot rod from Kansas, vroom, vroom.

I was ready to be entered and pleasured.

My body was to die for. Body fat probably 13 percent—sleek, velvety tan skin. My stomach was concave, nothing jiggled on this LA-faced, Kansas-bootied virgin.

For 2 years my high school boyfriend had tried to get in my pants. But those pants were steel clad and locked with an iron padlock, handmade by Lillian. The key was actually nonexistant. She figured after I married at age 28, she would then take a wax mold of my homemade chastity belt and at that time hand deliver the key to my eagerly awaiting husband, precisely 3 minutes after he said, "I do." Yes, that was Lillian's plan.

I had a different plan.

This high school boyfriend, let's call him Dick for short, although it wasn't . . . (God, how I love that joke.) This Dick, well he was without a doubt the most popular boy in high school. One of those bad-boy-slash-rebel types who, while the other cool guys were being pseudo hippies, was the awesome, cool, unique for the day "Marlboro Man." Denim shirts, long sideburns, knock 'em dead body—million dollar smile to top off his well-worn, very broken in roughed up suede cowboy boots. And, of course, he could play the guitar, sing like Paul McCartney, ride horses, scuba dive, and fly an airplane—and his family was very wealthy. They always ate prime rib instead of pot roast on Sundays. And here's the best thing, the very best thing, he had a monkey!

When he first asked me out, I feared that he was just fucking with my mind. I thought he and his also very groovy friends had one of those plans in mind where he picked me up, drove me to the country, they all jumped out, stripped me naked, and hung me in a tree. Sort of a *Carrie* kind of deal, but of course, even worse.

But then he did have a monkey, and Dick was, well, Dick, and every girl wanted a date with Dick, and who was I anyway?

I was a very goony girl who had gotten to be cheerleader because I could jump really, really high. There were two types of cheerleaders: the beautiful girls who secretly or not so secretly "put out," and then the minority of us—the girls who could jump really, really high.

My hair was still short, stupidly, ridiculously short, as Lillian had decided that my hair was way too thick and wavy to be long. And as we all know, thin, straight, slightly straggly hair is much more suited for long hair, right?

Anyhoo, I had the dumb hair and oh my, the really dumb clothes. Lillian made most of them—crotches-to-the-knees pants, designer dresses with the wrong fabric buttons and details. Lillian decided the "details" were of no importance and that polyester was a close runner-up to cashmere. My clothes were not only stupid, but so frumpy that I had to take a job at a clothing store to purchase store-bought clothes to destroy the hideous image Lillian had created.

Okay, so dumb hair, hideous clothes, no makeup!

This was a hard-and-fast rule in our house, devised by my beloved father. "No hair dyeing and no makeup. Women should be naturally beautiful."

Now, you know that's sort of swell advice to naturally beautiful women! I can think of five—Grace Kelly, Sophia Loren, Verna Lisi, Angelina Jolie, and Sharon Stone. So, dumb hair, hideous clothes, no makeup, and am a really, really good jumper.

So here is Mr. "I Can Get Any Woman in the Universe," and I choose . . . I choose, I choose you, yes you, the gooniest, most idiotic, badly dressed, shorthaired, high-jumping virgin to be my lawfully unwedded prom date!

How in the hell did that happen? I was the girl who also, unsurprisingly enough, wore a Dynel fall to school for a few weeks, pretending like it was research for an upcoming scene in drama class. I was the girl whose inner dialogue à la Carlos Castenada went something like this, 24-7:

I'm ugly, I'm stupid, I'm loony, I'm embarrassed, gee, I hope no one sees me walking down the hall. I'm flat, I'm a jock, I hate myself. Don't look at me, please look at me, no, don't.

Dick and I dated for 2 years. His frustration of not being able to fuck me mounted into a psychotic frenzy whereby he would drive away from my house laying about 50 feet of burning rubber, with a screech that would break a dog's eardrums.

So, due to knowing that Dick could no longer restrain his ejaculations and fearing, with the fear of a Christian around large felines, that it was merely a matter of days before he would explode or fuck another girl, I decided to let Dick have his way with me.

I weighed about 122 pounds, but deemed that 122 pounds was

not a fuckable weight. So in 1 week I dropped to 115 pounds (by eating only grape Jell-O and hard-boiled eggs).

My slut friend, call her Paula because that was her name, had advised me on a.) how to give head, b.) what sperm was, and c.) what "coming" meant. Her advice went something like this:

"You put Dick's dick in your mouth and swish it around a while, then he will start dry humping you, and then he will enter you. And you will need a rubber for that part because you don't want to get pregnant. You will really like it. Always have good manners and put the rubber on him and take the rubber off him, so he doesn't think you're an idiot who doesn't know what you're doing. When he comes, he will shoot out some sperm that will go into the rubber, so you don't have to worry about it sticking to you."

Sticking to me?

That thought worried me—"sticking to me." I didn't like sticky stuff. I still don't. Anyway, she did say I would like it, he would love it. And I was prepared by having my manners in check.

Dick and I drove up to this place by a creek where we used to make out. We began to make out in the front seat. It turned feverish. He hadn't gotten Paula's personal instruct, so he began to dry hump me first. This sort of threw a mental wrench into the mix for me, as sometimes dry humping could result in ejaculation, so I sort of brilliantly maneuvered him off me and unzipped his pants.

Oh, he must have been amazed because before this, "dry" was the only option. Out Dick's dick came and I took a deep breath and put it in my mouth and swished it around for about 20 seconds. Okay, check, good enough for the swishing. Now for the moment Dick's been waiting exactly 2 years for—voila—yes, Dick, it's true.

In my hand what you see is what you get, a bona fide, real lambskin Trojan rubber.

Dick was speechless, needless to say, and when he began to speak, I put my fingers gently over his lips (I'd seen some actress do this in some movie) and gently said, "Shhh . . . ."

I could tell by the look in Dick's dollar-sized eyes he was impressed. I fidgeted with the condom to get it open, but I don't think Dick saw. I rolled it onto Dick's dick with minimal awkwardness and then, the time had come for Kirstie Lou to become a full-fledged woman.

You'll like it. You're thin and beautiful. Your manners are good. He loves you. My whole life, my whole life I had waited for the man I loved to make love to me, and with a rapture of intensity I'd heard of, only from the likes of Romeo and Juliet or Lombard and Gable. I shall consummate this and explode with sensation.

He entered me—it didn't really hurt too much. He said he was being gentle as not to hurt me because I was a virgin. He sure knew a little too much about being gentle to virgins for my liking, but for now I would put that on the back burner.

I began to feel a tremendous sensation.

The sensation of feeling like I needed to pee.

Yes—I really had to urinate. The more he thrust, the more I had to pee.

Is this possible? Is it possible I've waited 17 years to experience a feeling I feel four to six times a day? A feeling I've felt since my first diapers?

His face was beside my face. The position I now know is the favorite assumed position by most men. Come on, they don't really give a fuck who you are as long as they are fucking someone. So the face beside the face—the effort position, I like to call it—is the winning position.

Sometimes I think that men place tiny little monitors behind our ears when we're lying there—a sort of computer screen that projects whatever fantasy woman's face is running through their minds at the time. And while we are in the final throes of lust and passion, they just stay fixated on their own personal portable semi-porn screen, which, of course, self-destructs the moment they ejaculate.

Dick was nearing the homestretch as I was still lamenting about needing to pee really badly, and wondering why this is what people really do to feel good, when making out and dry humping are much sexier.

I figure this whole scenario transpired in about 4 minutes.

In a burst of ecstasy, Dick was finished. I was numb. As his throbbing member shrunk inside me I felt . . . relief.

I didn't really have to pee after all.

But where are my manners?

I kissed Dick on the mouth and said, "That was the most amazing thing I've ever experienced." The first of many lies I would tell Dick and other dicks thereafter.

I took the rubber off his penis; I could feel the warm substance inside the condom. I was pretty sure this was the "sperm" Paula had warned me about. I was thankful that nothing sticky had gotten on me. As I lay reclined in the front seat of that Chevy Impala, I, with the manners to dazzle even Emily Post, tossed the rubber over my head and out the car window.

At least that's what I thought I'd done.

Rewind . . .

slow motion . . .

to . . .

I tossed the rubber over my right shoulder. I'd forgotten to roll down the window.

The rubber hit said window and ricocheted back, falling onto my face with a squishy plop. Sticky stuff was in my eyes, on my forehead, and on part of my nose.

Dick laughed.

I made a note to self.

Find a man who a.) looks at you when he comes, b.) doesn't make you feel like peeing, and c.) doesn't laugh at you for having good manners.

I'm still looking . . .

Baby wants a ride to school.

Did you say you wanted to party?

12 months after doing "it."

15

The Two Faces of Fat

Goodbye Baby

July 31st, 2004

Goodbye to good ole Maine and our sheep, Violet, Clover, and Sweet Pea. Looked spiffy with their newly shorn wool—sheared off yesterday to audience of 12 children and 5 adults. Goodbye to humping and bleeding, slip and slides, water trampolines, pies, cakes, cookies, wildflowers, and friends.

At airport noticed cover of People *magazine. Nice shot.*

Meet with Nate from Oprah show tomorrow in Los Angeles for kitchen remodel. Can't wait to stare at Nate. Might resort to random make-out session. Hope Oprah does not mind.

AUGUST 2ND, 2004

Met Nate at door—even more of a stunner in person. Wish was 25 again. Would bang Nate on front porch steps.

Children go with Parker for 4 weeks summer vacation. Saying goodbye painful. Always painful. Must feel same way to him.

Nate asks what hate and what love—then shoo shoo, off I go. Nate says with smile, "Kitchen officially off limits!" Wanted to make out with Nate even though 50, not 25.

AUGUST 6TH, 2004

Went to big Scientology mecca in Clearwater, Florida, called "Flag"—needed to answer question I'd been asked for past year and half, for self. Question was: "Well, when did you start getting fat, anyway?"

So, to Flag to discover for self when began to get fat. Scientology had, since 1979, been road to finding real answers for self about life. Perhaps once again will help lead me to road of truth and knock me off road to Enormous Assville.

AUGUST 10TH, 2004

Start special Dianetics sessions. Exciting. Only did Scientology sessions for last 15 years. Dianetics sessions will help get rid of unwanted attitudes, emotions, sensations, pains. Hoping unwanted fat might fall in category, too.

AUGUST 15TH, 2004

Dianetics awesome. Unveiling many years of occluded, painful emotions. Seems all of them were stuffed into ass, as ass seems to be shrinking along with painful emotions.

People have often, and I do mean often, asked me when I really started gaining weight. I've never told anyone, but I now know when it started and why. The gain began a long time ago, and just gradually got worse.

In 1990, I was pregnant and all was right with the universe. I was doing *Cheers,* I'd just finished *Look Who's Talking, Too,* and I was pregnant.

Most people don't know this about me, but I always yearned for children. I'd wanted babies since I was a baby. I used to say I wanted four boys and a girl.

But we screw things up in life sometimes, and boy, in this area I have really screwed things up. I've made many mistakes regarding this subject, and if I were to be perfectly honest, it is the only area of my life that I could be brought to regret about.

But now, I was pregnant. Somehow my universe had opened its arms to embrace my real dream.

At 3 months along, I had what is called a spontaneous abortion. That means the baby dies inside you. I found out this information at a routine checkup while getting a sonogram. There was just no heartbeat.

I was alone when I got this information. I was alone except for the thirtysome-odd million people who would read about it the day after, when I went to the hospital to have a D and C so that I wouldn't die of an infection.

Hospitals in Los Angeles have people on their staffs who call the *Star* or the other rags and tell such stories to them. Private, intimate stories of people's deepest pain and suffering.

So, the next day all 30 million and one of us knew I'd had a miscarriage. Only two of us were in pain, myself and my husband. It's hard to have a private pain that you are asked about by every passing stranger. You begin to create a real face answer and a false face answer.

This is the one devastating thing that has happened to me in my life that took years to recover from. Mainly because I would never confront it. Sure women have miscarriages every day. Some in the last trimester, or even more heartbreaking are those who have stillbirths. My 3-month miscarriage did not rank high in the ranks of female tragedy, however it ranked highest in the ranks of my own personal tragedy.

Bodies are funny things. These beings are inside you—unmistakably felt—and you begin to create the life and the dreams of a family together.

Why is it that crack whores can bang out kids like Pez dispensers and then there's me who did everything "right" and lost her child? What the hell did I do so wrong in the world to have that happen? The crack whore thing still bugs the hell out of me, to this day.

Anyway, the second I knew I was pregnant I began to get a little fat. And for the first time in my life and in my career, I *did not care.* All I cared about was a healthy, beautiful baby, so I ate and, yes, I ate too much. But I ate healthy food, too much healthy food, or just the right amount for being pregnant, I really didn't know. But I got bigger and bigger and bigger, and by the 3rd month, I had gained 25 pounds and I did not care.

I remember how I felt every day of that pregnancy, when I would wake up and realize that I was pregnant. I have rarely experienced that kind of joy.

When the baby was gone, I just didn't really get over it. Neither did my body. I so thoroughly convinced my body it was still pregnant that 9 months to the date of my getting pregnant, I had milk coming from my breasts. Like a false pregnantsy'd beagle.

I was still fat, I was still grieving, and I had just been told that it was very possible I would *never* be able to have children.

Fat, childless, with little hope for any future children . . . that's the real truth. That's when I began to get fat.

Six months ago I did a thing called Dianetics. Dianetics helps people get over losses and physical and emotional pains. I did these Dianetics processes, and within 2 weeks I had finally been relieved of all of my loss and pain connected with my failure to have children and the loss of that child. Thirty days later I decided to create a show called *Fat Actress*. I decided to take the onus off of something by out-creating it.

I decided to help people laugh at themselves so that they too might be helped to confront their own pains, losses, and demons. I decided to write this book then, too, in hopes that I could help other people, like myself, who've "gotten" in a certain condition to get themselves out of it.

So that's when I started getting fat and how I changed from "doing myself in" by continuing to get fat. So, now you know.

The best I could do was to tell you in my own words, and wish you children, family, love, and yes, food.

I, especially, wish you the ability to confront, discover, and change those things that have caused you your own personal pain and suffering.

I wish you truth.

Snap out of it!

Look what the future held for me!

16

"C.W."

AUGUST 18TH, 2004

Decide to have Italian night disco madness party to celebrate new revelations. Meet new foreign boy—boy is handsome, tall, smart, and 47—fair game.

Look smashing in ultra flat-ironed hair, sixties eyeliner, and tight, breast-revealing low-slung neckline. Boy notices me and shows lot of interest. For first time in 4½ years feel like flirting and have attention off ass, mind, and body.

Dance all night, then all jump in pool in clothes. Stars brightly glittering, lightning in distance, warm, clear pool water.

Lot of attention from many boys. Sleep well. Dozed off feeling for first time in many years, beautiful. Like there were still decent, kind, handsome men in world.

Could possibly now safely, educatedly, look for soul mate, if "soul mate" was not so grossly overused.

My grandfather was my favorite person. We were the true definition of soul mates. There was no doubt that out of the twenty-some odd grandchildren, I was his favorite.

And rightfully so.

I was the one who dreamed of owning a monkey that he had promised to buy me when I turned 8. And I was the one who spent her allowance on tiny Morton saltshakers to put on the tails of sparrows that we spent hours together trying to catch.

He enjoyed the same love of the unusual. So why wouldn't he favor the very unusual, eccentric second child of his movie star handsome son, Robert Alley?

I would spend the night at my grandfather's house as often as possible. He would give a dollar to whichever grandchild spent the night.

At one point around age 6, I began to question my own moral integrity, as I knew I did like that dollar. I wondered if I was such a conniving little temptress that the dollar was actually the real draw to Grandpa's house.

I decided to put my personal ethics to the test.

One Saturday night, while watching the fights at C.W. (Clifford William) Alley's house and drinking the tiny Pabst Blue Ribbon beer he'd prepared for me in a miniature shot glass with a pinch of salt on top, I said, "Grandpa, I want to stay all night with you a lot, but I don't want you to give me a dollar anymore."

You would have thought that I had just jammed a number two pencil into this man's heart. He welled up. He actually got tears in his eyes.

"I like to give you a dollar when you stay here—you might need it someday."

At that moment I realized that perhaps Grandpa Alley had been going through his own moral dilemma. Perhaps he wondered if he was "bribing" his grandchildren to stay all night. Maybe he worried that if he didn't pay us, we wouldn't be so eager to sit with him on a Saturday night and drink beer from thimbles. Or maybe he just worried that we wouldn't remember him at all if he didn't pay us to remember.

"Okay, I'll take the dollar, but you should know that I'd stay here even if you didn't give me a dollar."

"Thank you."

That Christmas the other grandchildren got bags of homemade noodles and socks and stuff, and I got a 3½-foot bride doll with a satin gown, real lace train, and shoes with pearls on them.

When I was 7, my grandfather had a heart attack while he was eating popcorn balls that my 10-year-old cousin Marilyn had made.

It was nothing short of murder in my opinion, but she was never formally charged.

I never did get a monkey or catch a sparrow with salt on its tail. But you know, I've settled the moral dilemma I had when I was 6.

The truth is, I'd give back all the dollars he gave me, and all the dollars I've earned since, to just have one more night watching the Saturday night fights and drinking a beer with my beloved grandfather, Clifford William Alley.

My hero.

My hero's peeps.

17

COCKTAIL ATTIRE

QUEERS AND ASSHOLES

AUGUST 30TH, 2004

Finished Dianetics program. Unreal realizations. Feel alive physically and no more unwanted painful emotions. Said goodbye to all Italian friends. Said goodbye to new prospect boy. Decided to seek out perfect diet program.

Decide to lose 65 pounds and to see prospective love interest in summer in Italy. Feels like brand-new life before me, and possibility of brand-new bottom behind me.

SEPTEMBER 2ND, 2004

Back in LA with children. So happy to be with children. Children comment on how good and happy I look. True asks if have found new boyfriend. Say no, but might have found potential soul mate. True laughs at stupid referral to soul mate, referencing overuse on The Bachelor.

Much business stuff. Wardrobe, locations, hair, makeup, lions and tigers and bears, oh my. New boy calls from Italy to see how things are.

New diet company approaches. Shakes—not my bag, no interest. Passadena.

Start shooting new show soon. Excitement building.

September 10th, 2004

Talked to John Travolta. Excited to do first Fat Actress *show. Laughed together about new rag story about how John has thrown in towel. Tired of hiring me chefs and trainers, giving up on my weight loss. John and I laugh 'til sick.*

Blake filming away on now meaningless documentary. Can't remember what documentary was about. New boy called from Spain—olé!

Get offer from little stupid diet company. Product sounds insane and pornographic. Also get offer to be spokesperson for big cookie company—tempting.

September 20th, 2004

First day filming Fat Actress. *Not nervous, exhilarated. Good friend, John, suppressed soul mate, friend, amazing actor, John, John, platonic love of my life, John. Oh, and also, new best friend, platonic love of life's wife, Kelly Preston.*

Brenda excellent, fun to work with. Felt like had taken 10 hits of speed, that much energy. God, I'm lucky.

Showtime made possible for me. Need to remind self to give head to Showtime head.

Need to thank entire universe for just being there. Can't express happiness in words.

Enormous ass invisible today.

OCTOBER 12TH, 2004

Kid Rock worked on show today. Tried to stay cool, didn't work. Wondered why Kid Rock said yes. Didn't really care, just happy he did. Dreamy, bedroom eyes, had enormous urge to fuck Kid's brains out. Wished was younger, skinnier, brain fucker. Kid Rock very funny, very sexy, wanted to have sex with belt buckle pressing against my—must shut up. Becoming delirious with notion of Kid Rock on top of Fat Actress. Delirious not policy, not prerequisite, for soul mate. Danger, danger Will Robinson. Not using "man of dreams," "soul mate" technology.

At 14 I'd saved enough money to send myself to Kansas University summer art school. I'd taught swimming lessons to kids from 1 to 3 years old to earn half the money. It wasn't that I really knew how to teach swimming to children, but I did know how to pry their little fingers off the edge of the pool and basically shove them into the water and yell, "Kick your feet!" This worked and I'm happy to say, I never lost a customer.

My parents paid the other half of the school tuition, and so there you had it, I was soon to be off to fine arts school for 3 months. But first, because the fancy art school brochure said "cocktail attire" for the "summer fling," which would be held the last Saturday of the summer, my dad and I went to find a "cocktail" dress at Lewins—a very snazzy dress store, the snazziest in Wichita.

When my dad took me shopping, which was twice in my life, I knew I would get something really wonderful. My mother was more concerned with "how much?" or "I could make that cheaper and stronger," or "oh no, it makes you look like a prostitute." Dad, on the other hand, just sat there and commented if he liked it and asked "Do you like it, Kirstie Lou?" The two times Dad took me shopping were both at Lewins. Lewins had a salon. The husbands or dads would sit on a peach-colored velvet sofa, and the grand dames of commission would choose the dresses they thought appropriate for you from the back room full of apparently appropriate semi-coutures.

These dresses were not being "given away," as I still like to say. They ranged from a thoughtful $200, upwards to around $1,000. This was a very long time ago, so these dresses were pricey and unique.

I tried all sorts of appropriate dresses on and thought all of them looked too childish. Kirstie Lou wanted something sophisticated, yet young, groovy, and heartbreakingly sexy. This was my big chance to shine, my coming out. I was going *away* to fine arts school where *no one* knew me. *No one* knew my geeky past, *no one* knew I wasn't brilliant, and *no one* knew I was a virgin who still played with her Peanuts collection of Schroeder and Baby Sally and Sherry Lewis's Charlie Horse and Lambchop. I would be anonymous—mysterious and, quite frankly, downright elusive.

But look—there it was. The dress that would make all the others pale in comparison. Ice blue, green, purple paisley. Giant paisley. Silk empire bodice. Short. Very short mini dress with the same sheer pattern chiffon on its billowy sleeves. Wide scooped neck and buttons covered with silk all the way down the back and eight covered silk buttons at the wrists. I really do believe it was one of a kind. Most of the salon dresses were. But one of a kind was not such a commodity in those days.

It transformed me as I put it on. The further I pulled it up over my body, the less of an idiot I became, and when the final button was buttoned, even I thought I was stunning. I had to look at myself in that salon mirror for a good long time. It just wasn't real that Kirstie Lou could look like this, and I looked skinny, really skinny. Long beautiful legs. I noticed slight cleavage from the very modest empire scoop. My hair was short but it fit—like Suzanne Pleshette or Twiggy.

When I walked out from behind the velvet curtains, my dad beamed a huge smile at me.

"That's beautiful," he said. "You are beautiful in that dress. What do you think, Kirstie Lou?"

Green kid-leather shoes to match—exquisite. Dangling, pale-blue drop earrings with drops the size of marbles, not some dainty little girl's earrings. The new me, phantom goddess of art school, earrings.

The entire package must have cost my dad a full $600. It was our unspoken secret . . . until now.

This trousseau gave me the courage to venture from home, something I'd never done for more than one night, and become the artist, the woman, I wanted to be.

Art school was composed of music, ballet, painting, and sculpture. It was also composed of primarily street-savvy, much more mature teens than myself. The teens ranged from age 14 to 18. A large span of growing time, experience and life, between the two ends.

Did I mention I was dense? Extremely. Not worldly at all.

Other than my newly acquired fashion trousseau, I was green, green, green. All these "teens" were a handsome, beautiful, eclectic mish-mash of artistic bliss.

I was intimidated by them, of course. They were everything I wasn't. Until I saw Jeffrey, spelled Geoffrey—6 feet, 3 inches; dazzling cobalt blue eyes; black, thick poetry hair. Geoffrey was poetry, a Renaissance man right there in front of me at Kansas University. I'd never seen a human being this extraordinarily beautiful. Tony Curtis looked very good, but not this good.

In my mind I had children with Geoffrey and we lived in New York City. I was a very well received painter, and Geoffrey performed at Radio City Music Hall. Did I mention that Geoffrey was a ballet dancer? Anyway, our children had blue eyes, and everyone commented, "How could two people as beautiful as you have anything less than the most stunning children?"

Geoffrey chatted with me every day for a week. Smart, articulate, can't-catch-my-breath handsome Geoffrey. He likes me.

He would seek me out. I could tell how much I meant to him.

On Saturday, Linda B., this girl who made her own bell-bottoms and crop tops (but really, really well)—had at least 50 outfits by count—was kind enough to tell me that Geoffrey was going back to New York City on Monday. That Geoffrey had been going to Kansas University all year, and that Geoffrey was just at summer art school to finish out Geoffrey's last semester . . . oh, and also, Geoffrey is a queer.

I said, "Queer?"

"As a three dollar bill," Linda B. said.

This is where my greenness shone through, like the North Star. Hard to imagine these days, but I had not a clue what "a queer" meant, not a clue. I didn't even know for sure that three dollar bills weren't in existence, frankly.

"A queer?"

"Yes, you know, a homo."

Ah, yes, "a homo." Not a clue what "a homo" meant either. *A homo sapiens, a homo erectus? A homo away from homo?*

"Yes, you know, he likes boys, not girls!"

This was the moment in my life when I learned that some men liked men more than they liked women.

Later that night, Linda B. and her 18-year-old roommate Mary were even kinder to tell me exactly *how* Geoffrey would be liking men more than women. And to top it off, as a hard-and-fast rule, they warned me that "all ballet dancers are queers."

"Remember that Kirstie, all of them, so don't bother to fall for them."

Bam, one-fourth of the population of art school became off-limits because I, of course, summarized that the ballerinas were also queers and would soon be coming after me.

Geoffrey did break a tiny corner off of my heart, but it was well worth the future life lesson . . .

Dancers are queers, keep your distance. My giant paisleyed dress would not be worn for beautiful, smart, queer Geoffrey. I cried anyway when he left.

In the next weeks, art was hard and art school was harder. I was amongst some truly gifted artists. Sadly, I was not one of them. My oil painting instructor instructed me to keep scraping the oil paint off of my canvas and begin again. I used the same canvas the entire 3 months. That's the beauty of oil paints, they take forever to dry—not so water color, at which I was equally untalented. And not so sculpting, at which I was strictly amateur in comparison to my counterparts.

In short, I had no talent as an artist, and in fact it left me wondering what the hell I was even doing at a fine art school. All those tiny fingers pried off the edge of the pool, and for what?

Then I saw Ken. Not drop-dead gorgeous, but cool looking. Sort of Ben Affleck cool looking—big smile, very, very funny. Everyone loved Ken. A guy's guy and a girl's heartthrob. If I wasn't talented (and I definitely wasn't), at least I was meant to have a good time, find true love, dance, kiss, and get serious. Just like all those beach movies. Just like Butch Cassidy and the Sundance Kid, with Kathryn Ross, kissing, dancing, loving.

This was my new purpose at art school, to conquer and please Ken. Ken was a, not queer, guitar player.

I knew it would take some doing. Many girls were after Ken. I needed to hip up the hip factor. I began to borrow Linda B.'s clothes. Every day a cool new costume. They were tight, but I thought that was a plus point.

I wore more black eyeliner. I laughed more at Ken's group jokes. When he made eye contact with me, I would hold his gaze. I would not look away. Just like in the movies.

One night, right after dinner, Ken swooped by and said, "Kirstie, meet me in front of the dorm around 9:00. I want to ask you something."

I wasn't stupid! Of course he wasn't going to ask me to marry him or even go steady, but no doubt he definitely was going to ask me to the "semi-formal, cocktail-attired" end-of-summer fling.

He would ask and I would blushingly accept, and that would be that. And we had 4 weeks left, so we would make out every night, and I might smoke for the first time, and he would cry when my parents came to pick me up to take me home, and we would see each other every summer at art school and then attend Kansas University together. He'd graduate 3 years before but attend grad school as I finished up college, until we both graduated and got married and told jokes all the time.

Nine o'clock sharp, I was prompt. He was even prompter. He was waiting for me. A few of his friends were sitting on the steps a few yards away. I approached.

"Hi Kirstie, glad you came. I want to ask you something."

Yes, Ken, I'll marry you and bear your sons.

"Here goes, I want to ask you to ask me to kiss you."

"What?"

"Yes, I want you to say, 'Ken, will you kiss me?' And then I'll kiss you."

I began to speak, to ask . . .

"No, no, no, first get on your knees, then ask me." Big, beautiful smile, deep dimples, piercing into my soul.

As I nestled down onto my knees, I thought, *It's quirky, but romantic and wild. I like this new game.*

"Ken," I giggled, "Ken, will you kiss me?" (And then take me to the dance and then go steady and pin me to be engaged for 4 years, then marry me and grow old together?) I didn't break my gaze, I held fast to his gaze, lover to lover, soon-to-be "cocktail" attire to cocktail attire. Big smile, dimples as deep as the Grand Canyon.

"No Kirstie, I won't kiss you . . . but thanks for asking."

The nearby friends broke into a cackling pack of hyenas. Ken began laughing as if a frenzy had overtaken his soul, slapping his leg, flashing that huge, beautiful smile.

And then a familiar face appeared.

Linda B. came strolling around the corner. Ken swung his arm around her shoulder, and she yelled over her shoulder to me, "Don't forget to bring back my clothes tonight . . . Cinderella."

They howled as they rounded the corner of the ancient, ivy-covered dormitory. I stayed on my knees for a few minutes, not knowing how I would ever face anyone again and knowing that the jig was up. They all knew me now and knew that I was *not* mysterious, not elusive. I was as much a fool as I'd always been, back in Wichita.

For the next 4 weeks, I pretty much spent my time looking at the ground and scraping my oil painting.

The night of the summer fling finally arrived. My cocktail dress was on, my earrings were glittery, my green kid-leather shoes were perfect. My hosiery was pale ice blue, slightly shimmering, a sparkling, exquisite pair of hosiery. I was, however, numb, not there, not glistening or perfect or exquisite, I was hollow.

I went with a guy who had a crush on me, but to me he was just a friend. We didn't stay long; we came back and changed into jeans and shirts. I liked the way my heavy eyeliner looked with casual clothes and decided to always wear jeans, white cotton shirts, and a lot of black eyeliner in the future.

We hung out and walked and talked about our time at art school then went down by an old bridge. This guy Percy was on the railing. He said he was going to kill himself. Everyone was horrified and petrified. Ken, Linda B., Mary, all of them were riveted to his threat. Percy was pumping his potential suicide for all it was worth, wringing every drop of sympathy and pathos out of each bystander.

Do it, go ahead and just do it. You think the rest of us haven't been through anything awful? You think we've never felt any pain? You think your heart aches more than ours do?

I'm tired. I'm tired of being stupid and naïve. I'm tired of loving queers and assholes. I'm tired of art school and of being a bad artist and mostly I'm tired of desperately trying to get people to love me—especially men—so, go ahead and jump, Percy. Jump off the fucking bridge. Represent, represent for all the assholes everywhere who have broken young girls' hearts for sport. Do it, Percy. Jump off the bridge in your "cocktail" attire so that this summer fling will tattoo itself on our minds forever.

He never did jump, which, in a way, is too bad. It would have made a much better story.

But in memory of dear Percy, in case he ever did get the balls to do it, and as a gentle word of warning to all you "Kens" of the world: Be sparing of young girls' fragile hearts, for those young girls do grow up, a little worse for wear, and sooner or later one of them will not only break your blackened heart but will rip it from your bloody, gaping chest and chop it in an automatic vegematic and serve it to your sorry ass for dinner.

Cheerfully, Ken old boy, I hope this has been your destiny.

Buon appétito.

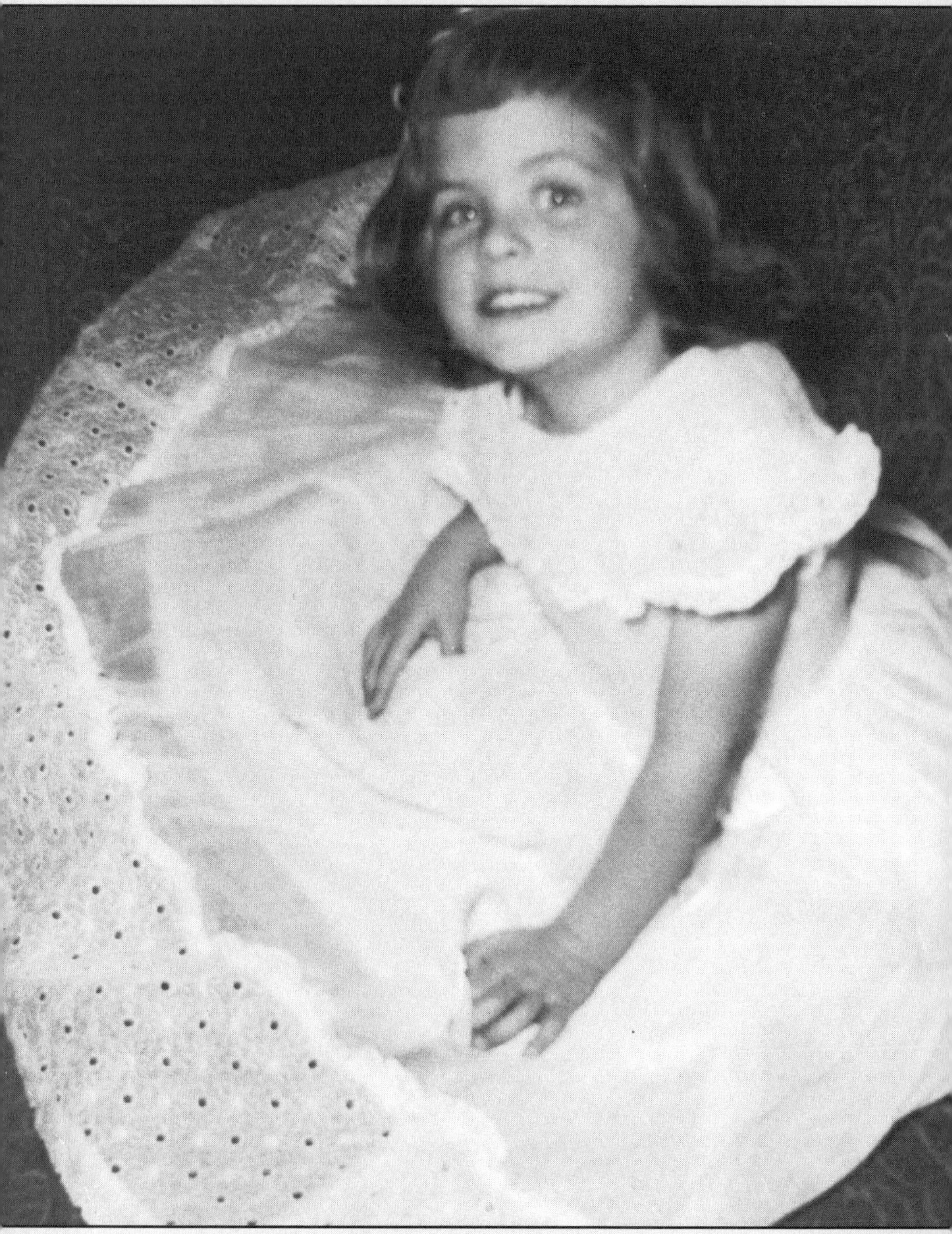

Hello Ken, is that your heart I see dangling from your neck?

Top: Bobby—not a queer—sorry I can't say the same for my hair.

Bottom: Vintage Dior, queerly fabulous!

18

The Two Faces of Fat

Hello Christmas

October 16th, 2004

Put up Halloween decoration in new basement kitchen, living in for months because of Oprah/Nate makeover. Giant spider on wall with giant black tape cobweb. Long-time assistant LeeAnn decides to move on to new occupation. Very sad day for me, LeeAnn has been by side 14 years, like sister, best friend, partner. LeeAnn decides to stay until January 1st, 2005, this gives comfort. Happy for her, her real love is to have hair salon. Want her to have her real love—she deserves it. Thinking lately, also deserve real love for self.

October 29th, 2004

Nate came to reveal kitchen to me. Astonished at beauty and style of kitchen. Eternally grateful to Oprah, who makes all wishes come true. Oprah is closest thing to Santa in USA. Couldn't wait to get to Chicago to thank Oprah in person. Still want to make out with Nate, but now for different reason. Want to thank him for new kitchen with token sex acts.

NOVEMBER 1ST, 2004

Fly to Chicago to do Oprah *show. Have new, handmade suit. Hair and makeup artist friends flying in to Chicago from New York. New suit made old ass look smaller and younger. New boots, too—Yves St. Laurent. Very stylish, reach to knees and have little French heel.*

Flight was flight from hell, like twilight zone. Whole flight in storm. Almost had nervous breakdown. Ate huge meal in hotel when landed. Ate another huge meal before bed. Another in bed.

Did Oprah *show. Felt like made two new friends, Oprah and Lesia, producer on* Oprah *show. Felt easy and natural. Excited to give Oprah first exclusive on-air interview since announcement of show. Knew she understood abundant rump.*

Left for noodle-house restaurant, joined by New York friends and Lesia. Noodle house good.

NOVEMBER 3RD, 2004

Check self into swanky Four Seasons hotel in Chicago. Decide to hole up in suite and give up smoking cold turkey.

No smoking today but ate like horse—horses. Got message from home, foreign boy had called to check in. Did not care. Too pissy to talk to anyone. Acted like asshole until nightfall.

Then acted like asshole in dream. Then woke up acting like asshole, like serial killer.

Glad Four Seasons has Bible in drawer, not 45.

NOVEMBER 5TH, 2004

Craziness subsiding. Decide to go shop and buy Nate thank you gift. Look for antique Hermès pieces. Apparently no antique Hermès pieces in Chicago. End up buying 10 cashmere scarves served up in stainless steel colander.

Had Nate, Nate's mother, and friend of Nate's, Fernando, by for pajama party, dinner, and movie watching. Provided Nate, Fernando, and mom with fuzzy dog slippers. All showed up in pajamas. Dined on every item listed on room service menu and some made up by selves.

Nate and Fernando spoke of exotic trip to Indonesia over Christmas. Laughed about Nate preferring "five-star hotel" camping to "tiki hut" camping.

Eenie meanie, miney mo, hmmmm . . . now want to make out with Nate and *Fernando . . . separately, of course.*

NOVEMBER 6TH, 2004

Travel back to LA, still no smoking. Flight smooth. No desire to murder people. Happy with Oprah *show, happy to see children, happy to get back to filming, happy to move out of basement.*

Agent called and said Jenny Craig people want to meet with me at end of month. I accept. True agrees to do episode of Fat Actress *to play snitch to rag mags. Lillie announces she will never do episode of* Fat Actress*, has no interest in child acting. Kids and I begin planning for Thanksgiving. Decide to have Robin and Art and kids as guests. Suggest* *leave their corgi Lizzy in Kansas. Kids order turkey-shaped cakes for friends for Thanksgiving. Is Dad's birthday, sent him gift, called him in Kansas, told him loved him.*

Celebrate his birthday here in LA by taking kids to dinner at Acapulco Mexican restaurant. Fifteen tortillas and 750 nachos later, drove back to house and collapsed on sofa eating chicken-flavored Top Ramen.

NOVEMBER 25TH, 2004

Thanksgiving painfully fun. Ate, ate, and ate, then went to fancy restaurant and ate. Back to house and new kitchen and several thousand cookies. Ate dessert of pumpkin pie, pecan pie, hot fudge sundaes, and turkey cake. Later in evening, snacked on sausage gravy and biscuits and Pillsbury croissants.

Gave thanks for children and prayed to close new Jenny Craig deal to become spokesperson before eating self to death.

DECEMBER 12TH, 2004

Make decision to eat all food in world to prepare for massive Jenny Craig weight loss. Spend each minute with Lillie and True before they go to Parker's house for Christmas. His turn this year. Oh, and new boy called. He'd like to come to visit in February. Think I'll let him.

DECEMBER 18TH, 2004

Children go to school and then go to Parker for first part of Christmas vacation. We cry saying goodbye. Lillie and True invite me to dinner on Christmas. I accept. Send them on way and proceed to eat everything in Nate's new kitchen.

There are many fun ways to gain weight but bar none, the most fun, the grand-daddy of all food fests is, unequivocally, Christmas.

Eating and sex sort of reside in the same time zone. Either can be abused and become devastating, or can be used successfully for survival and extraordinary pleasure. The most fun eating is with people you love on a holiday. I love to cook for people. I love to razzle-dazzle them with my culinary delights. I love Christmas cooking most of all.

I think I learned this from my grandmother, Annabelle. Every holiday, but especially Christmas, she made the most visually tempting and yummy concoctions I've ever experienced.

Like great big Santa cookies. These were sugar cookie Santa heads with beautiful handmade frosting detail. Blue eyes, white frosty beard, eyebrows and hat trimmed with finely grated coconut atop white frosting, with pink cheeks, red hat, and intricate detail to make the blue eyes twinkle. I've never had such beautiful cookies since.

Those were my favorite part of Christmas. The time that Annabelle put into each cookie. Can you imagine? Probably at least 20 minutes per cookie, only to be gobbled up in about 30 seconds. I guess the Santa heads were the size of my adult hand.

Next came her homemade chicken and noodles:

Eggs, salt, pepper, flour, and a touch of cream "with as much flour as you can get in there," then roll it out fairly thin with a rolling pin. Then take these flat, approximately 12- by 12-inch pancakes, roll them up, then slice them up into one-quarter-inch strips. Fluff them all up with more flour, lay them out to dry, and begin the chicken.

Get a *very* fat stewing hen, throw it into a giant pot, throw in salt and pepper, a couple of carrots (for flavor), celery stalk, and onion. Boil this for 2 or 3 or 4 hours. Take the chicken out, followed by the vegetables. Let the vegetables cool off, then give them to your dogs.

If you have company, dice *only* the white meat to go back in the pot. Never, ever, ever, even if the Russians are holding you hostage at gunpoint, ever give dark meat to guests. It means you can't afford to be selective.

This was a notion Annabelle had, left over from the Depression. You know, the real Depression of 1938, not the current everybody's-depressed-and-needs-anti-depressants "depression." The real one where people had real things to struggle through: droughts and dust bowls and plagues and locusts and such.

Anyway, don't give dark meat to guests. Give it to your own children in the privacy of your own home the following day.

This will make a clear, beautiful, yellow, fattening, glittery chicken broth. Rich with the dark meat flavor, but not with its apparent poverty-revealing nasty-colored meat. Now as the broth boils, drop the homemade noodles in.

Not in one big dump!

No, they will all stick together, and you'll join the ranks of currently "depressed" people and you, yourself, will have to reach for the Prozac. No, no, no, drop them in respectfully in a manner so that each gets its chance to hit the boiling broth and dance for at least one second.

Now that all the dancers are snuggling in their brew, turn the fire to simmer and stir them on and off, but more on than off, so that they don't stick and burn. In about 20 minutes you will have something not short of paradise—homemade chicken and noodles.

Pecan pie also played a role in the event. And if you want good pecan pie, use the recipe from the back of a Karo syrup bottle.

Don't get fancy, I hate fancy, don't fuck it up with chocolate chips, fake pecans, or cream cheese. Just follow the fucking recipe on the Karo syrup bottle and it won't fail.

The same with fudge—just look on the back of the marshmallow fluff jar. That's the best fudge recipe in the world. Why candy companies fuck around and try to improve it, I'll never know, when the magic is right there at their fingertips.

Annabelle also made green bean casserole, scalloped potatoes, mashed potatoes, sweet potatoes, candied sweet potatoes, boiled new potatoes, dressing, turkey, ham, and roast beef, two to three kinds of gravy, homemade biscuits, dinner rolls, pies, cakes, snickerdoodles, Russian tea cakes, and 10 other types of cookies. Oh, and I shouldn't forget the ribbon candy, gum drops, jelly beans, and my personal favorite—candied apples.

During these feasts, I'd feel more peaceful and cozy than a Norman Rockwell painting that had a sleigh wreck with a Courier and Ives litho. Of course, if Annabelle was a great cook and everyone else around had been assholes, the memories might take on a different spin . . . but I testify here and now, not much of a spin! Those colors and smells and flavors and the abundance of artistic delight would have given me pleasure even if I'd been dining with the likes of Howard Stern.

I was always torn between orgasmic bliss and deep-seated shame that I was privy to such a feast while all the "pagan babies" we had collected money for in Sunday school were starving somewhere in Africa or Borneo. The only way I momentarily made it all right to indulge was by convincing myself that I literally could not mail the food to Africa or Borneo, but I could give more money at

Sunday school to ensure that "pagan babies" did not go without.

I remember the sounds of my cousins laughing and screaming, stories being told, bragging, our snorting at bad jokes, and cousins flirting with cousins—an incestuous holiday indulgence. Annabelle, not accepting help from any of the other 10 women present, slapping anyone's hands who came near one of her steaming delicacies prior to "dinnertime."

And then it would happen, that second in time when all is right with the universe.

Annabelle would come into the living room, which was probably only 20 feet from the small-housed kitchen. Nevertheless she made an entrance worthy of Julia Child.

"Dinnertime!"

The dining room was filled with all the cousins, moms and dads, aunts and uncles, plates clanking, more laughter, compliments flying to Annabelle. Kudos made to the Queen of Holiday Cooking. More laughter, more pervy flirting, eating, complimenting, eating, laughing, flirting, eating . . .

This is what I remember about holiday food. This is how I remember Christmas as a child. This is how it became fun for me to eat too much.

Top: Do you have any cookies? Or are you just gonna stare at me?

Bottom: Look what Santa brought me!

Is dinner ready yet?

19

LORD JIM

December 25th, 2004

Christmas—washed hair, put makeup on, went to Parker's house for Christmas dinner. He served goose and turkey, mashed chestnuts and yams. His mother was there from Pennsylvania. Was lovely occasion, felt fortunate to have all together.

Played with children and their new toys. Kissed children goodbye, wished all "Merry Christmas."

Came home, finished wrapping and delivering gifts, setting up Lillie's new doll house and True's new paintball equipment. Headed to Matterhorn Chef restaurant to have second dinner with friend Colleen and family. Ate my way across Switzerland.

Returned to house to show off new Nate kitchen and play Cranium with Colleen's children. Watched It's a Wonderful Life, *realized I'd reached my goal made 1 year prior, to find out how to reduce ass and create wonderful life for self and others.*

This was Christmas gift to self.

Sugar plums danced in my head until I reached up, grabbed one, and ate it.

Note to self: now that know how to reduce ass, start doing so soon.

December 26th, 2004

Children came back to me for my portion of Christmas vacation.

They shrieked with astonishment at their gifts, so generous themselves, so thankful for what they have. Made me remember how I'd grown up. My mother and grandparents, now gone.

Proud of children for being themselves and being so gracious.

Went back to Matterhorn Chef for round two of Swiss feast. Had to show True and Lillie this treasure of restaurant. Parker, his mother, and new girlfriend joined us. Girl he used to flirt with on Baywatch *and deny flirtation. Made me feel better about all actors I'd flirted with throughout marriage.*

Thought how circular life is and how weird to have accordion player banging out medley from Sound of Music *while reflecting on old times. Left Matterhorn, took children to see Christmas lights on Candy Cane Lane.*

Snuggled in bed, children in arms again. Merry Christmas to all and to all a good night . . . . However, did need to creep downstairs to help Santa fill stockings. Santa kind enough to come back to our house on the 26th.

December 27th, 2004

Got word of tsunami in Sri Lanka. Got word that Nate was in Sri Lanka as planned, for Christmas with friend, Fernando. Nate can't find Fernando. We pray for them both. For them all. Tried to keep some dignity while praying.

This boy Jim fell in love with me the minute he laid eyes on me. One of those obvious crushes that you pray for after age 40.

He followed me like a puppy from room to room. He would call me nightly and have his mother say to me, "You are *muy linda*" (very pretty) and other love talk in Spanish. I guess Jim figured a foreign language would razzle-dazzle me, especially there in the heartland of Kansas.

He used to tell me how beautiful I was—sweet for a boy of 10, which is how old Jim and I were when he came a courtin'. To be so pure that he had no inhibition about speaking his mind.

He loved me so strongly and so thoroughly that it left me no choice other than . . . to . . . play impossibly hard to get and basically, sporadically, completely uninterested. Like at the skating rink on Saturdays. It was a given that the more gaga Jim was over me, the more I was forced to flirt with Jim's older brother Hale.

Don't get me wrong, I wanted to love Jim as solidly and openly as he loved me, but loyalty and devotion just weren't in my makeup at that early age. I was boy crazed as hell, but interested in random boys, drive-bys, like Steve U., Steve S., Larry C., Jamie K., Bobby R. Every other day I loved a new one.

Hell, I just didn't trust myself to come up to the mark young Jim had set at this early prepubescent age.

A few years passed, but not Jim's love for me.

It was an "on" period for me. I was being kind to Jim and loving him back. He was 12 now, and much more interesting. Jim's family was extremely wealthy. They owned a huge construction company in Wichita, Kansas. They lived in a huge mansion, belonged to the country club, and had a "children's line."

Today, lots of kids have phones in their rooms, cell phones, and even private lines, but in "old school" days, kids beat the hell out of each other to talk on the telephone, and only really rich families had private lines for their children. They were listed just like this in the phone book:

Dr. E. L. Richypants—murray42586

Children's line—murray42587

Jim called and asked me to meet him at "fun night" that coming Saturday at his swanky private school, Collegiate. Jim said he and Eddie would be there early, so could I be early, too? Eddie was Jim's best friend, from an even wealthier family. Eddie's family lived in a historic landmark, a Frank Lloyd Wright house. Eddie had this beauty queen mother, extraordinarily beautiful, like a movie star.

My best friend Becky went to Collegiate also. I think all the rich people including Jim's family and Becky's family all got together and built the private school so that their kids could be properly, privately educated. Anyway, I was in cahoots with all these rich folks because I was on the Wichita Swim Club. Swim club was half bijillionaires, one-quarter po' folk, and one-quarter almost po' folk, otherwise known as middle class. That was us.

I'd already planned to spend the night with Becky and go to Collegiate's fun night with Becky and Jennifer, another really rich kid whose mother I later worked for as a maid. Maid Kirstie ended up driving Becky and Jennifer and various other rich girls to the "club" for summer swims, while Maid Kirstie scrubbed Jennifer's mama's house till it shined.

We all showed up for "fun night," and most of the boys sort of shucked and jived and oh gosh'd the girls. But Jim was different, he came right up to me and said, "You wanta go swing?"

Swing, of course, meant sit on the swings and talk, and hopefully kiss, which is what we were doing for about an hour—all of the above.

Be still my playgirl heart. Tonight, I am as smitten with Jim as he is with me. Or so I thought 'til Devil Girl arrived . . . .

Jim was wearing a beautiful gold watch. I was admiring it, mostly so that I could touch him more. I was holding his arm, admiring his watch, when suddenly Devil Girl must have risen up from hallowed earth and erupted inside me.

My burning love for Jim turned to evil intentions.

"Oh yes, this watch is beautiful Jimmy boy, it's a real beauty. Is it a Twistoflex?"

Twistoflex was a newly invented watch of the sixties, with a very limber, highly flexible wristband. I knew in my heart and brain that this watch was indeed *not* a Twistoflex, but with Satan lurking in my psyche, I had no will of my own.

"Jim, let me see your watch."

He slipped it from his wrist.

"What a beautiful watch, Jim," I said, softly, coyly, like sugar butter soup.

Jim cooed and looked dovelike into my eyes as I admired his beautiful gold watch—and then, snap, like a horse's neck at a rodeo.

"Jim, is this a Twistoflex?"

I grabbed the band with both hands and maniacally twisted the watch into a mangled pretzel, crackle-twist, twist, tork, crackle, crackle. There. The princess of darkness had done her work.

As quickly as I'd snapped into the Antichrist, I snapped back. And there was Jim, looking shocked, like a rabbit caught in a flashlight. His beautiful, contorted gold watch lay in the palm of his hand, where I'd quickly deposited it after my "fit."

No words would or could be spoken for several minutes.

"You nut," he said, finally. "Certifiable."

He began to laugh.

"You're out of your mind. That's why . . . I love you."

Oh my lord, why can't I find a Jim these days? A Jim who thinks I'm gorgeous and extraordinary even when I'm in the middle of a demonically induced grand mal seizure?

We had so much fun that night at "fun night." He was my hero. I would love Jim forever and never again flirt with his brother Hale . . . until the following Saturday at the skating rink.

And this is how it went for the next 2 years. His love for me was overwhelming, and the more I tried to love him back as strongly, the more I triggered the diabolical spirit within my soul, and I would do or say something ridiculous to spoil it and push him away.

Not that he ever faltered or fell back, but that was definitely Ms. Satan's intention.

Jim was a handsome boy, really handsome with blue eyes and dark hair, beautiful teeth, and a wonderful smile. That's why it's hard to believe that right in the middle of madly making out in a field behind the swim club pool, I took the opportunity to trip Jim and wrestle him to the ground, screaming and teasing that he was the only boy I'd ever kissed who insisted on wearing really pointy-toed Beatle boots!

Wild with laughter, I yelled out. "Beatle shoes, Beatle shoes, Jim Richie wears Beatle shoes!"

And then the time when Jim and Eddie walked out of a drugstore, and I couldn't pass up the opportunity to yell, "Beatle shoes, hey Beatle shoes! Where's Paul and Ringo? Ha, ha, ha, ha, ha."

God, I was funny, witty. Damn, I should be on TV.

Hale got a crush on my sister, and that pretty much ruined the brother flirt thing for me. Besides, I was starting really to fall in love with Jim. I'd not made fun of him, broken any of his possessions, or tripped him in months.

I hadn't laughed like a hyena at his shoes in weeks.

My resistance was crumbling, my demon was quieting.

One weekend, Jim said he was going camping with Eddie at the ranch and that he would call me Monday. They were going on a survival weekend, very macho, very male. That was fine with me. I was supposed to babysit the kids across the street on Saturday anyway, and their mom didn't like me tying up the phone line.

Jennifer called me Saturday morning.

"You don't need to come and clean my mom's house today. Oh, and by the way, guess who's dead?"

"I don't know, who?"

"Jim and Eddie. Jim and Eddie are dead. They got asphyxiated last night at the ranch."

To this day I can't believe the note of unimportance in Jennifer's voice when she relayed their deaths to me. The glibness and casualness of her demeanor was haunting.

"Gotta go now. Are you okay?"

"Oh yes, I'm fine, goodbye."

Children walk around like zombies just like adults do after death. It feels like someone has hit you with something really hard, right between your eyes, stunning you into numbness and unreality. I stumbled around this way all day and into the night.

I was lying on the sofa, while babysitting across the street, when the nightly news came on. My charges were long since asleep, so I was alone when the story of Jim and Eddie was broadcast. As the reporter smirked and told the story of the two Wichita boys from prominent Wichita families, the film footage began to show two bodies being carried from the little shack where Jim and Eddie had holed up that night and lit the gas stove for heat on their macho survival trip.

The faulty gas stove with no safety in case the flame went out.

You couldn't identify which was Jim and which was Eddie. Blankets were over their bodies, but then I saw and then I knew. The very bad Beatle boots were peeking out from one of the blankets.

I thought I, myself, would die that night. Partly because of lost love and partly because of all of the stupid, mean, evil, thoughtless things I'd done to Jim during our 4-year love affair.

I didn't stop crying until the double funeral for Jim and Eddie. Double caskets, double families, double friends, and double priests. Eddie's mother wore a black dress, black stockings, gloves, and bag, and a big, black hat with a black veil. She nearly fainted several times as she walked down the long aisle of the Catholic church. Men flanked her and caught her at each fainting falter.

Jim's mother, by contrast, was dressed in a cream-colored suit. Her hair was styled, yet simple. She had a lovely handbag, and she smiled a lovely, soft smile as she walked down the aisle to her family's place.

She emanated something very powerful—hope and spirituality and knowledge. A certainty that life does not end when our fragile bodies do.

She taught me a great lesson that day. Not of death and loss and grieving, but of love and faith and life. One of the most beautiful lessons I have learned this lifetime.

I'll never forget the contrast between Eddie's mother and Jim's, between death and life. Jim's mama was radiant in her faith.

You are *muy linda,* I thought, sending those thoughts telepathically to Mrs. Richie that day.

You are truly *muy linda.*

Jim, sorry about the watch—oh, and P.S.: Lose the shoes!

I think of you often . . . These are my kids, the same ages as us when we fell in love.

20

POOPING

December 28th, 2004

Film Jenny Craig commercial. Have been eating Jenny food for few days now. Lillie came to set with me. True stayed at home to play paintball with friend Cyrus.

Shoot goes very well. People very nice. Food very delicious, especially fettuccine.

December 30th, 2004

Drive to Oregon with kids. Land at ranch tired and dirty. Check out horses. Go to store and buy supplies. All eat Jenny Craig chicken fettuccine for dinner, with salad and soup, then snack on Jenny popcorn and cheese curls until bedtime.

Forgot to drink enough water for last 3 days. Need to . . . well . . . poop.

I had been prompted by my yoga teacher, Steve, to ingest large amounts of an herbal laxative called Cascara Sagrada. At the time I had gained 15 pounds and weighed a whopping 140.

Unfortunately, throughout my life my motto has always been "more is better," so "large amounts" was interpreted as enormous amounts.

There's a big freeway in LA called the 101. It's very congested and very big. As I sailed along the 101 with my 4-month-old daughter, Lillie, and my 2-year-old son, True, "In the Evening," by Led Zeppelin, my favorite song of all time, blasted on the radio. I remember feeling like I was the luckiest person on Earth. Led Zeppelin in my ears, and my children, future Led Zeppeliners, behind me strapped safely in their car seats.

The sky was purple-blue, I was in great shape, my body looked like a goddess. But I just wasn't quite skinny enough. I was driving home from the set of a movie. I had the cake and the icing too, and I knew it.

Suddenly, my stomach began to cramp—the kind of cramp that would make a man go in for surgery. At first I thought I was going to pass a kidney stone, or worse, die of a burst appendix. Then I felt a deep rumbling in my lower intestinal region that was pressing against my . . . well . . . butt.

I remembered this feeling from when I was 3 and I'd intentionally pooped in the bathtub with my sister, Collette. She used to ignore me, and as Glenn Close said in *Fatal Attraction,* "I will not be ignored." I deduced that bathtub pooping was a surefire show-stopping attention-getter. I was correct.

At first I was pretty casual about the impending poopathon.

I'll just ride it out. I've only got six more exits.

But then the traffic began to slow, and then get even slower, as is the case every day at 5:00 on the 101 freeway.

Have you ever had to poop so badly that even the thought of fluffing put the fear of God in you—lest you messily soil yourself in the attempt?

My father was sick only one day that I can remember in my whole childhood. This day was significant, as my father came home at noon, something he never did, "to change his clothes," my mother said.

I was home sick with the flu, when he walked into my room and said, "Kirstie Lou, I'll let you in on a little secret. Your ole dad pooped his pants at work today."

That's really why he was home changing his clothes. After he headed back to work, I began to laugh. "My dad pooped his pants." It didn't get much funnier than that, and I took solace in the fact that even dads pooped their pants now and then.

The solace and humor had subsided that day on the 101 as I realized that True and Lillie's mother, Kirstie Lou, was about to poop her own pants.

A plan, a plan, I need an excellent plan . . . and quick, I thought, clenching my ass as tightly as I could, which was tighter than a Princeton pledge at a hazing.

I had it!

Oh yes, a marvelous plan.

I recalled a gas station off the next exit.

I'll bolt in there and unload my Cascara Sagrada–induced toxins. Yes, yes. Great idea. Good thinking in a pinch.

As I exited the 101 on Havenhurst, it suddenly dawned on me that I couldn't possibly open my car door, open the back door, undo two baby car seats, grab a 4-month-old and a toddler, and "bolt" anywhere, let alone a gas station toilet where I'd probably have to ask for a key from some illegal alien at the inside counter before I could enter the restroom anyway.

I'll leave the kids in the car and just run in. I'll park the car just outside the door so that nothing can happen to them. And I'll lock all the doors.

Funny how these "thoughts" conjure up all car nappings, ad infinitum, in the entire universe. And after all, nothing pisses me off more than people who leave their kids in cars and then say on the 11:00 news, "I just left him in the car for 30 seconds while I ran in to get my dry cleaning, or some milk, or drop off the dog."

And what was I going to say on the 11:00 news?

"I just left them in the car for 30 seconds while I ran in and shit my brains out?!"

Actually, there is something that pisses me off even more than car nappings. And that's that inevitable group of people who live in trailer parks in Kansas.

Again, if I've heard it once, I've heard it 20 times a year for as long as I've lived. "Yeah, we heard the sirens and we seen the tornado, but we didn't know it was gonna hit us. We don't got a house no more, we don't got nothin."

I don't even feel sympathy for these idiots anymore. And I believe God put them on this planet to make the rest of us idiots feel smart.

So, no "bolting" to the restroom with or without my children was feasible. But Mount St. Kirstina was moments away from erupting.

The sweat was pouring down my face, the pain unbearable.

I watched as my hand, independently, reached into my baby's diaper bag, grabbed a Pamper's, and shoved it down my pants, nestling it beside my tight little ass. And as I watched this, I thought in slow motion, "Wow—what a brilliant idea. I wish I'd thought of that."

Some say cathartic moments happen only a few times in each lifetime. This was one of those blessed moments. An explosion of great magnitude occurred. But I felt protected, joyous, invincible really.

I pulled into my driveway, opened my door, opened the back door, undid both car seats, put my shoulder bag over my shoulder, grabbed both babies, and proudly walked into the house, past my housekeeper, my husband, and the painter, who were none the wiser.

I was not on the 11:00 news that night crying about my missing children or wondering how my double-wide got twisted into a knot. I was cradled snugly in my bed, with my babies beside me . . . who never would know that on her way back from work one day, their mama had pooped her pants and saved them from kidnappers and tornados.

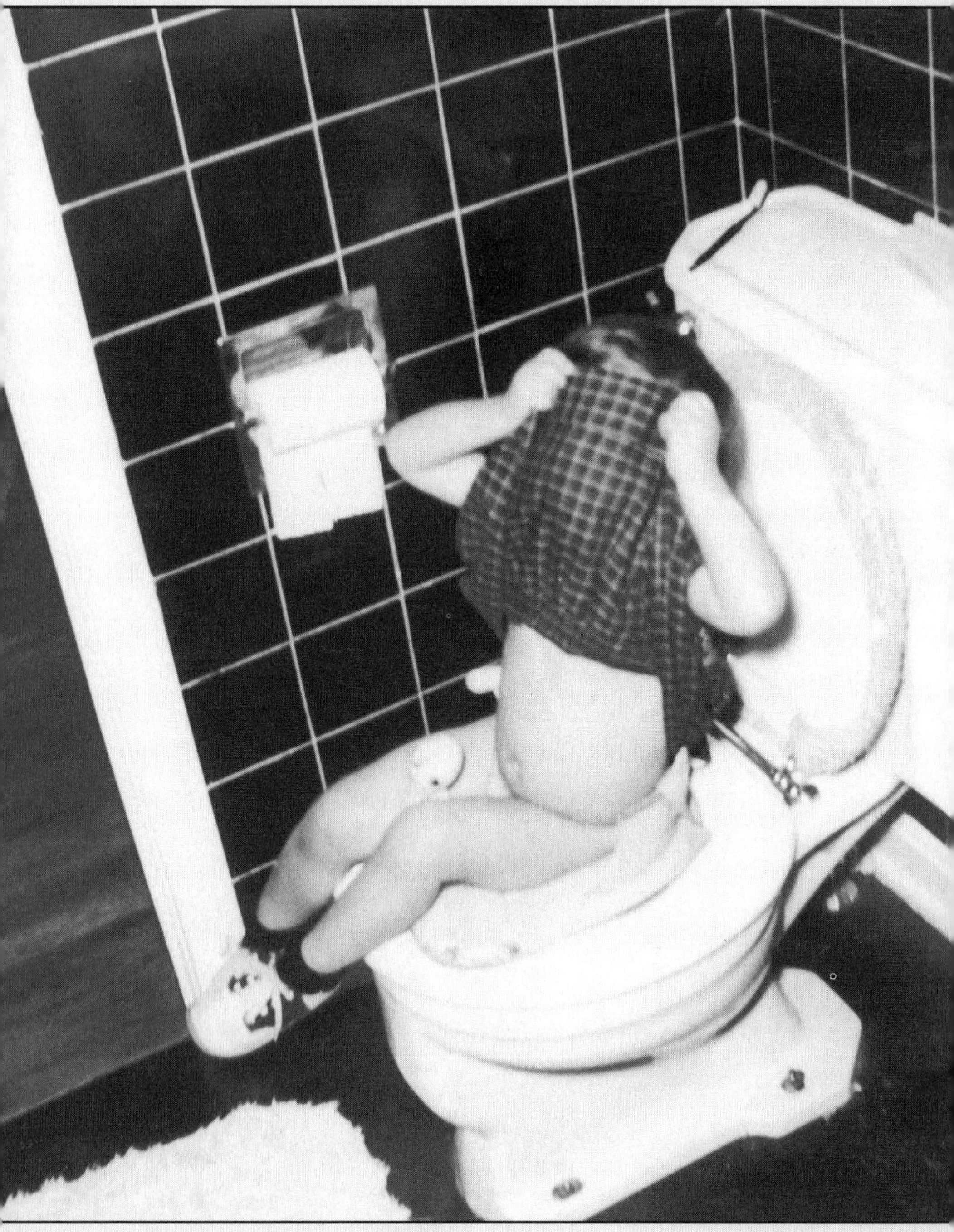

No officer, I'm not the lady who left her kids in the car to go poop.

I'll give you back the key when I'm finished! Jeez . . .

December 31st, 2004

New Year's Eve. Made giant bonfire in forest in Oregon with True and Lillie. Snowing out when we torched the pine pyre. Danced with children for hours around fire. Good exercise. Excellent experience.

Pulled car up close to fire and opened all doors and blared Santana. Santana—great fire-dancing music.

Forgot to make New Year's resolution. Too consumed in wonderment of my beautiful, dancing children.

January 1st, 2005

Woke up, looked at past year, and wept. For all I had, for all I'd been through, for all I'd seen others go through, and for all that was in our futures.

I knew my ass was soon to be lost, and I knew, without a shadow of a doubt, that I had a beautiful life.

So here's a heads-up to any of you who might be contemplating becoming a fatty like me. It really isn't worth it, and society will not be kind.

Social brutality is the stock and trade of fatty haters.

You will be shunned and scorned and looked upon as less. You will be gossiped about and treated as though you are lazy. You will mysteriously lose out on the best jobs and the most attractive, wealthy mates. In fact you won't need anyone else to screw you, you will be expertly screwing yourself.

I know it isn't fair or correct, but it is true—with few exceptions.

If there's one thing I've learned in the last few years about getting fat, it's that—I screwed myself—no one had a gun to my head; true, fatty-haters had their fingers poised on the trigger, but I held the gun.

I also held the happiness.

Happiness is within all of us, and that's the only place we'll ever find it. So we might as well put our attention to the beautiful things of life—loving people, helping people, and changing ourselves to make our actions more effective and more useful.

Haters will always be haters no matter what they hate us for. Our color, our sexuality, our politics, or our religion. We need do nothing other than . . . keep loving them.

And go about our business of making this a better world for all of us, and for all of our unique and varied asses.

So here's to asses everywhere
Some are waxed and some have hair
Most are hefty, some are small
Some are giant and some are tall
Here's to asses, north and south
Here's to asses, inside and out
Here's to butts, buns, and booty
Cheers to bottoms all powdered and fruity
Touch them, smack them, get to know one
Asses friendly, even 'ho ones
Black or red, white or brown
Ass is queen
Our reigning crown
Here's to asses all day long
Muscled, sculpted, weak, or strong
When all is said of pomp and class
Our common link's
Our fresh cracked ass